RESTORING
VIRTUE

RESTORING VIRTUE

a testimony of HEALING through the
ATONEMENT OF JESUS CHRIST

EMILY HOPE

PRINT ISBN 13: 978-1516896479
PRINT ISBN 10: 1516896475

Interior designed by Gated Publishing.
Cover photo: ©megapixl.com/6905234.
Edited by Belliston Editing Services.

CONTENTS

A WORD FROM THE AUTHOR

The purpose of this book is not for family members, friends, or anyone who has crossed my path to feel regret for the past, nor is this book to make the reader feel sorrowful. It's not meant to be a platform for past sins and misdeeds. This is not a cry for help as I have made a full recovery. Lastly, this book is not meant to create or pass judgment upon anyone referenced within its pages.

The issues I talk about affects both men and women, but I am writing from a female perspective and out of concern for the virtue of women.

All names have been changed or excluded except my own. The reader would benefit from refraining to identify the characters. This is just someone, somewhere with a story. My narrative is not meant to be traumatic, but some who have never been exposed to any type of abuse may find it to be. Other victims may experience triggers of their own abuse, but if they are committed to the healing process, they will also experience hope. Details are kept to a minimum; however, my words are not meant for young children.

This is a story about how my religious beliefs helped me overcome the effects of sexual abuse. The things written in this book are my own thoughts, ideas, and insights based on the testimony I gained. They are not endorsed by The Church of Jesus Christ of Latter-day Saints. More information about the church can be found at lds.org or mormon.org. A request can be made for a free Book of Mormon or for contact information of local LDS missionaries. Terminology common to the LDS community is used throughout this book. A glossary at the end is for readers who are unfamiliar with these terms.

I have wrestled a great deal with the decision to publish—how I portray the people who influenced my life experiences, and how the things I share will affect them. I've refrained from telling other's perspectives as much as possible and only when it directly relates to my story. It's important for the reader to understand this is my truth, my pains, and my testimony. However, this book tells only the smallest fraction of my life experiences. It will give a small glimpse into my heart, but barely touches the surface of my story that runs deep both in sorrow and in joy.

Sometimes words are hard to find for rich life experiences. I've done my best to find the right words to tell this story. If my words fall short, it's only by my natural weakness, not a lack of conviction.

This book *is* to bear testimony of the Atonement of Jesus Christ. The backstory and past experiences are shared in order to show the distance traveled, give hope for the future, and to testify that *all* can be restored.

My hope is that the reader will gain a greater testimony of the power of the Atonement to heal all wounds.

For the word of the Lord is truth, and whatsoever is truth is
light, and whatsoever is light is Spirit, even the Spirit of
Jesus Christ. And the Spirit giveth light to every man that
cometh into the world; and the Spirit enlighteneth every man
through the world, that hearkeneth to the voice of the Spirit.
Doctrine and Covenants 84:45-46

Emilism: My inner voice or the Light of Christ.
My compass.
My guide.

INTRODUCTION

*For behold, this is my work and my glory—to bring to pass
the immortality and eternal life of man.*
Moses 1:39

Emilism: I am living proof of the healing power of the
Atonement of Jesus Christ

My name is Emily. I was a victim of childhood sexual abuse
and its devastating consequences. Countless times I wondered
who I would have become if my life had not been altered by
these traumatic events. I struggled for years, not ready to let go
of the victim inside. The experience gave me depth and
uniqueness. I had a story to tell. But the story I'm telling now is
more powerful than the victim's story. It's a story about the
Atonement of Jesus Christ. It's a story about God.

I do not claim to be any kind of scholar. In fact, I've never
been to a day of college in my life. I'm not older or wiser—the
truth is I still have much to learn, but I'm opening my
heart

and telling this story to bear testimony with the hope I might be able to light the way for someone else. It is based on my own experiences, past journals, and memories. It's authentic and as true as my memory allows.

Mine is not the most dramatic story; however, it is the most common story—the kind that runs rampant throughout our society. Childhood memories shrouded in darkness, conflict, and strife. Stories of abuse swept under the rug, of families in denial, simply afraid to face feelings of failure. Victims whose voices are silenced, and as a result abandon their efforts to heal and turn to addiction for relief.

What makes my story unique is how I paved my own path to healing—a path less traveled. I labored and toiled and reaped the reward. I worked hard for my own peace, happiness, and healing. It did not happen all at once, but it led me to God and to the Atonement of Jesus Christ.

Through my honest search for a true relationship with my Savior and Father in Heaven, I made the discovery of a lifetime. This discovery actually covers many lifetimes. It is true and eternal and there for all who are willing to come unto Him.

It is that God's children are His treasure. My path not only led to God, but to understand my divine worth and recognize the light within.

For God, who commanded the light to shine out of darkness, hath shined in our hearts, to give the light of the knowledge of the glory of God in the face of Jesus Christ. But we have this treasure in earthen vessel, that the excellency of the power may be of God.
2 Corinthians 4:6-7

Along my search, I carried with me my greatest wish: that I might know true happiness. As I stumbled through life this desire influenced each decision I faced. I wasn't going to let anyone destroy my chance for happiness, not even myself! I've been called stubborn many times. Regardless, that personality trait saved me in the end. Of all the times, I wanted to quit, there was always that little bit of fight that wouldn't let me give up.

PART 1

CHAPTER 1

And this is life eternal, that they might know thee the only true God, and Jesus Christ, whom thou hast sent.
John 17:3

Emilism: Writing is the voice of my spirit.

This morning I awoke to find my orchid ready to bloom. A petal had lifted on a bud hanging from the long spike. I've watched it grow, day by day, while I sit next to the window where the sun nourishes its leaves, writing this story—the journal of my life.

It's been some time since my orchid was active. As the buds matured, I mistakenly expected the flower inside to be pink. Instead, the soft white sheen of the petals blends in with the floating snow on the other side of the windowsill and the drifts collecting on the peaks of the mountains. Set against this peaceful backdrop, my orchid is a simple reminder of virtue and purity.

The thick green roots that produced this bloom twist and turn under a pile of messy bark. They remain hidden, tucked away in a white ceramic pot. The roots are not a characteristic to be admired, but they are the essential foundation of this plant. The bloom is simply a by-product of their complex design.

Journaling is a skill I acquired through years of diligent practice. The consistent recording of life events, experiences, feelings, and lessons became the foundation for this story. For someone who does not take time to look past my cover, they may see the appearance of a perfect life. However, these pages reveal a different story, one of how, like the delicate orchid, my life emerged from beneath the darkness, blooming with restored virtue.

As a child I was terribly sensitive and shy, which caused me some discomfort, but overall, I was happy and healthy. My introverted personality caused me to avoid drawing attention to myself. I rarely spoke up about anything and always had a desire to be good. Being number three in a family of one boy followed by four girls, this is what some people would consider typical of the middle child.

I ran around with the other kids in my neighborhood, riding bikes and jumping through sprinklers. There were late night slumber parties with girl talk, ghost stories, and silly pranks. I learned to swim at a young age and loved the water, practically living in a bathing suit. Much of my childhood was spent on a swim team and playing in my backyard pool. When my parents bought a baby grand piano, it was delivered to the formal living room of our house. I eagerly began lessons and spent hours behind the black lacquered instrument. Since then, music has been a huge influence in my life. School was not difficult academically, but I was not the smartest kid in the class either. Working hard to get good grades paid off when I graduated high school with honors.

Although my childhood was filled with many activities, home was my favorite place to be. I'm still a homebody and love the idea of home being a place that offers peace for all who live within its walls.

I see myself as a good mix of my parents' personalities. As a child, every time I heard the jingle of my mother's car keys, I jumped up to follow wherever she went. I was a mama's girl through and through. She is blessed to be a nurturer and devotes her life to being a mother and wife. She finds satisfaction in taking care of all the people around her.

My dad is an intellectual, and it's rare to see any emotion from him. A surgeon by profession, he obtained three college degrees and education is very important. He approaches life in a practical way and is always aware of things he believes to be right and good. He also devotes his life to taking care of our family.

I have much to learn from both my parents, and they gave me many happy memories. They love me and through all the ups and downs of life they did their best. When two young companions dream of building a life together with a happy family, they don't think to prepare for tragedy.

As a mother now, I give age-appropriate information to my children about their bodies. The way our society is today, you must keep this line of communication open. Children are inundated with messages about sex and body image. They need protection and proper instruction given in love. For whatever reasons, more than twenty-five years ago, my parents did not see the need to have this kind of discussion with me. As a result, my first introduction to anything sexual was by my older brother in the late hours of the night. I can't tell you exactly when it started, but I can tell you when it ended and what happened in between.

Emilism: Secrets destroy relationships.

Soft flannel sheets, light blue with a small sheep print, dressed my white wrought iron daybed. Lying there, I watched the sky through the shutters that covered the window just above me. Most nights the sky was completely clear in my small southern California farming town, so it was exciting when a storm would blow through. I learned to love the sound of rain hitting the window, as it was a rare thrill.

Life was a simple routine of attending elementary school until one seemingly insignificant night. I woke with a jolt as someone pulled my underwear down to my knees and pushed their hand between my legs. My body tensed and I kept my eyes shut tight. The world stood still, frozen in my mind.

The intruder left and a short time later, my brother, five years older, came into my room along with my sister, just two years older. I do believe she was unaware of what took place that night, and the role she was manipulated into playing. Nevertheless, the following experience broke my faith in the one thing every child inherently has faith in: the safety of my home.

I sat up as my siblings approached the side of my bed. With the night's darkness surrounding the secrecy of our conversation, they told me they had seen an intruder break into our home. "Has someone been in your room too?" they asked. "Yes, yes," I confirmed, terrified to reveal more. I put my trust in my big brother when he promised that together we would set out to discover the perpetrator. There seemed to be no need to include our parents in this plan.

The next day at school, I sat in my steel-constructed desk imagining myself a detective as I looked around at all the boys in my class with suspicion. When I walked in my front door at the end of the school day, I immediately approached my brother. "When are we going to search out the intruder?" I prodded. He didn't say a word. He didn't acknowledge my question or even look at me. His silence crushed me and I decided then that I was alone in the world.

The following night the intruder returned. With feelings of isolation creeping in, I surrendered to my fate. Once the surrender took place, next came shame, then guilt, and finally fear.

I don't know how long I believed someone was continually breaking into my home to violate me. However, I do vaguely remember the night I realized it was my very own brother. Knowing my abuser was a member of my family brought the violation to a whole new level and my isolation was solidified.

Both our rooms were at the end of a long hallway in our ranch-style home. It was easy for secrecy to be maintained.

My mom took advantage of the quiet evenings after her five children were tucked away in their rooms. Most nights I could hear the television going as she caught up on her daily chores. With my brother kneeling by the side of my bed, I heard her soft footsteps coming down the long hallway. A few more and she would be at my door. Quickly, my brother jumped up and pulled the covers up over my naked body as I lay stiff as a board. He ran into the bathroom attached to my bedroom and closed the door quietly behind him. For my mom, entering the dark room, there would have been no sign of trouble. She flipped the closet light on and hung the freshly washed clothes. Keeping my eyes shut tight, I remember wondering what would happen if she came to my bed and pulled back my covers, making the discovery of her life. I wondered if I would get in trouble. The light flipped off and my mom left. My brother came back to my bed to pull my underwear back into place, as if nothing had been disturbed, before retreating across the hall.

As encounters with my brother escalated, I had no idea what parts were what. All took place in the late hours of the night. I never opened my eyes and there was never a word exchanged. I pretended to be asleep: my best and only solution, my only defense. In reality, I was only fooling myself.

I crawled into bed every night dreading his arrival and hoping the morning might bring an undisturbed sleep. Those less fortunate nights, when I awoke to the touch of his hands, my heart would sink deep into my chest and my mind silently cried: *Just leave me alone.* My little heart raced at every intrusive touch and I felt suffocated under the weight of his body.

When the coast was clear, I would tiptoe to the bathroom, close the door quietly behind me, and flip on the light. These were the only moments, when I finally opened my eyes and saw my reflection in the mirror, that I connected with the reality of what was happening.

Quietly getting back under my covers, I curled up on my sheets to avoid the wet marks he had left behind.

My emotions spiraled out of control. I was depressed, I hated myself and anxiety settled into my heart. Some mornings as I stood at the corner waiting for the school bus, I imagined walking out into the street and letting a car hit me. *What would it feel like?* I wondered. *Would anyone care?* I shielded my eyes from the bright sun as I watched a gray sedan speed by. *I missed my chance.* The yellow bus approached and my mind moved on to thinking of the day ahead.

Almost imperceptibly, a dark shadow was cast upon my life and my emotional development was brought to a standstill. At this point the Emily that could have been was gone. A child's mind is a vast, impressionable place waiting and yearning to be filled, hopefully with love and guidance, but too often it is filled with other devastating experiences. I don't know which of my emotions were normal growing pains that every child faces and which ones were a direct result of the abuse. Even if the thought ever occurred to me to tell, I don't know if I would have had the words to do so. Abuse, suicide, and depression were not part of my vocabulary.

I was twelve years and four months old when my family moved from our home in the small farming town to the big city two hours away. The moving truck, weighed down by my family's belongings, sputtered up a steep grade through the rocky mountain pass. I stared out the window hoping this bumpy truck ride was my escape.

CHAPTER 2

For I reckon that the sufferings of this present time are not worthy to be compared with the glory which shall be revealed in us.

Romans 8:18

Emilism: Lies break hearts, truth heals them.

After my family moved into our new home it seemed like I was free from my brother's pursuits. My white daybed was dressed with new sheets and placed in the security of a bedroom across from my parents' master suite. Drifting off into my mind's world of secrets, I thought of my brother, alone, in a more isolated part of the house. Occupying the only bedroom on the first floor, I didn't think he would risk being caught creeping up the curved staircase that separated us. While deep in thought the song "I'm Gonna Be (500 Miles)," sung by The Proclaimers, played on my small alarm clock radio. I hate that song now. It still sends a chill through my neck and pulls me back to that room, as a young girl with a terrible secret.

A new school meant new friends. I received an invite to a boy-girl birthday party. My parents would have objected to the Spin the Bottle game, but the parents of the birthday girl looked on without any disapproval. The kids who were not part of the game danced to music coming from the boombox. I stood next to a long table covered with snacks. I'm sure I looked like the loaner and was an easy target. A girl approached me and teased, "I told Toby you wanted to dance with him." My breath stopped short in my throat. I was humiliated, but there was no time to think because Toby was walking towards me. I didn't want to dance with him, and not just with him, not with any boy—I hated boys. All my hidden emotions came spilling out in one hard swing as I punched Toby in the stomach. I turned and ran as tears welled up in my eyes.

The party was still young, so my mom was surprised to hear my voice on the other end of the phone demanding to be picked up. I pulled the handle on the car door, but I wouldn't look at her when I got in. When she expressed concern about what happened, I clammed up and refused to speak.

My actions that night raised a huge red flag, and it wasn't the last. Those flags popped up any time I had a negative encounter with a male and confirmed my growing belief that men could not be trusted. It didn't help that my relationship with my dad was pretty much nonexistent. He worked out of town and was only home on weekends, essentially leaving my mom alone to raise us kids. I didn't have anything to counteract these negative male influences.

I began fixating on my body. I wanted to be skinny, but was never fat. I took a seat at the green picnic table at the edge of the school quad. The sun shone through the tops of the trees, but I never opened my lunch bag. The food in it may have quenched my physical hunger, but the emotional hunger was stronger—the hunger for control. I lost about ten pounds within a few months. My mom took notice and commented on my slimmer figure. At first it didn't appear to be a serious problem, so I continued to dabble with food control as a way to express the feelings I could not give voice to.

During my freshman year of high school, my family took a week-long vacation to Hawaii. We stayed with my aunt and uncle on the North Shore. Their back door was just a few feet from the soft sand. I spent hours snorkeling, looking through the coral reefs for exotic fish. With the sun on my back, my skin turned darker day by day, complementing my wavy blonde hair. On rainy days, I wandered through small gift shops with my mom looking at small Hawaiian treasures.

At night, my parents slept on the pull-out bed in the living room and us kids in sleeping bags on the floor. With my parents a few feet away, my relaxing vacation came to an end when my brother reached into my sleeping bag. My eyes popped open in shock when I felt his hand touch the edge of my pajama bottoms. Either I was a little smarter or my anger was building, but I clamped my legs together and wouldn't budge. He couldn't put up much of a fight as our entire family was around us and eventually gave up.

The next day I did everything I could to avoid him. The sun set behind the blue ocean waves and the family was gathering inside, but all I wanted was isolation. I walked a fair distance down the beach until I saw a wooded area. I found a place to hide in the curve of a tropical tree trunk. I let my emotions suffocate me while I listened to the sound of the crashing waves.

Roughly two years had elapsed between encounters, creating a false sense of security. Some untouched space in my mind spent those years carefully forming a dark cloud. I visualized my life on a timeline with the abuse trapped in this dark cloud, looming over my "real" memories. I imagined my future, living out the rest of my life with this closely protected secret, but was not sure what that life would look like. Maybe at some point the cloud would just detach and float away, no longer casting its shadow. But this present encounter abruptly brought me back to reality. Nothing had changed. My cloud would not go away, but only grow darker and more terrible.

Emilism: God gave me a heart and it's a good one.

My high school swim team was one of the only things that brought some life into my world. When I put my head in the water there was silence and the whole world disappeared. It was just me, the splashing water, and the sound of my own breath. I worked hard and during my sophomore year and won the Junior Varsity league title in the 100-meter backstroke.

That day the swimmer in the lane next to me was expected to win. She was taller, stronger, and had a better recorded time. With a few encouraging words from my coach, I jumped in the water and held tight to the starting block. When the horn blew, I cut through the water, light as air. At the last flip turn I knew the title was mine. Several yards separated me from the girl in the next lane and I touched the wall, bringing in my personal best time.

I burst with pride when my coach hung the first-place medal around my neck.

That same year I met my future husband at the church building where we attended early morning seminary. None of the scriptural lessons stuck, but it was not a total waste because meeting Tom in the hall changed me forever. He was seventeen years old.

He wore a white Wonder Bread T-shirt and green Converse shoes laced up the sides, almost always with a beanie over his long brown hair and a smile on his face. He was popular, cute, and funny. Everyone loved Tom.

One morning as Tom pulled away in his father's white station wagon, he called to me, "Hey, Emily!" as he threw a note out the window. It landed on the ground and I walked into the parking lot to pick it up. On the front it said, "I like you a lot, babe." Inside he wrote how much he liked me and thought I was so cute. I read that note and fell head over heels.

My parents didn't let me date yet, so once a month we met at church dances held in the gymnasium. The DJ played the song "More Than Words" by Extreme. Tom took my hand and guided me through the crowd to the center basketball ring. Through his permanent smile he told me, "This is our special spot because you're special." His words peeled my heart open—wide open. I felt like the center of the world there in the center of the floor. Having his arms around me felt comfortable and familiar. In his arms was the only place I felt like I belonged. He was the first boy to reach into my hurting soul. We finished our dance while he sang the words of "our" song.

Later that evening we stood together on the manicured lawn of the church. My freshly opened heart pounded as he leaned in to give me my first kiss. It would prove to be the most memorable kiss of my life.

Our church congregations buzzed with excitement because the prophet, President Gordon B. Hinckley, was scheduled to speak at a regional youth conference. Kids were camped out on the lawn all day to get good seats. I wasn't one of them. However, circumstances allowed for me to sit next to my future husband in front of the doors where the prophet would enter. In respect, the congregation stood upon his arrival. The doors opened and without hesitation Tom grabbed him in a big bear hug. I'm not sure if the prophet was startled, but he hugged Tom back. Before he continued on, the prophet extended his hand to me.

Maybe it was just my imagination, but as we shook hands our eyes met and I wondered if he could see right through my soul. All my mixed emotions from the abuse were tightly bottled up. I wondered if this great man of God saw anything special in me, or if there was anything special about me at all. The young man sitting next to me thought I was special, and that was good enough for the moment.

Unfortunately, my relationship with Tom did not last long because of our age difference. Two months after my first kiss Tom left me standing on the steps in front of the church and it was clear there would be no more notes, dances, or songs to be sung. Every night for the next year I drifted to sleep, missing Tom's presence. A hole was left where he had opened my heart that no one else could fill. Even though I went on to date other people, I never let go of my feelings for him.

Two more years came and went—another two years of secrets. The first time I told anyone about the abuse I was sixteen years old.

Jess approached me after an assembly held in our high school library. He had long dark hair and was the star soccer player. He never reached into my heart the way Tom did, but I found comfort in our relationship. He was an outlet for many of the feelings I couldn't express, and I was more open with Jess than anyone else up to this point. A year into dating I decided it was safe to share my secret.

The conversation we had while sitting in my red pickup truck was short. He seemed concerned, but never suggested taking any action or telling anyone else. Surprisingly, nothing changed after these words were spoken. No release or revelation, no comforting feeling. But it did bind me to Jess in a particular way.

Our relationship ran its course. We grew apart and broke up just before graduation. My secret remained intact as I put on my white robe and cap to accept my diploma.

One month later I clocked in for my first day of beauty school. Now old enough to attend the young single adult ward, many of the boys liked to use cheesy beauty school pick-up lines on me. When asked, I agreed to go out with one of these young men.

Nate and I were never a couple, so I'm not sure why I felt comfortable confiding in him after a handful of dates. The pressure of this secret was building and I was having a hard time keeping it in, but I wasn't prepared for the solution he gave me. "You have to tell your parents." *Have to?* I thought. *No way, I am the one in control here.* Any feelings of attraction were immediately replaced with anger. It was as if he took my two realities and declared war. This shock to my system was more than I could take. I promptly cut him out of my life, and again, my secret remained intact.

Nate was right, of course. My parents needed to know, for so many reasons—mainly for the healing process to begin.

I didn't care one bit about Nate's feelings, or how hard it must have been to carry the burden of my secret. My anger towards him was unjustified because, in truth, he did me a great service. For the first time, I began to contemplate a future without the secret.

The internal battle had begun.

I was asked out by another young man. Ryan was not my type, but all the other girls drooled over his height and large muscles. I figured: *Everyone else is dying to date him. Why not give him a chance?*

I had some practice, so this time it wasn't as hard to share my secret past. The battle was already raging, so when Ryan also encouraged me to tell my parents, it didn't come as a shock. It was also much easier to take in because Ryan knew it was my decision and didn't place any pressure on me. "When you're ready I'll be there for you—110%." In the end, though, his influence wasn't the reason I decided to break my silence.

Both my older siblings had left the nest and were out pursuing their own futures. So when my family gathered for dinner on a warm October Sunday, we were absent two members. Admittedly, having my brother gone brought some sense of peace back into my home life.

"I have something to share," my dad announced. He had been hired by a hospital in another state, a much colder state than I had known growing up in sunny California. In three weeks, he would leave and my mom would follow with my two little sisters after the house sold. Armed with this new information, I realized time with my parents was limited. My chance to tell was now, never, or I didn't know when.

The six years before I told my secret felt like a waste. So much learning, growing, and preparation happens between the ages of twelve and eighteen. Instead I simply went through the motions: weekly church attendance, regular family nights, consistent family prayer, youth activities, seminary, even completing the Personal Progress program. All this while managing to not gain one ounce of a testimony.

My biggest regret in life is the loss of those precious, impressionable years to a nothingness inside myself. I shut out the world and withdrew. In a city surrounded by millions of people, I was utterly alone.

CHAPTER 3

Casting all your care upon him; for he careth for you.
1 Peter 5:7

Emilism: Healing takes place in honest hearts.

Although I told three people before my parents, I hadn't told the right people. It still felt like a secret because I continued to live the lie. I felt its weight, but had no intention of stepping out of the shadow. I thought of these three people as my secret keepers: people who I used to unburden myself without any thought of the consequences.

Of course, there was another person who knew. There was no need for words with my brother because fear bonded this secret between us. For him, there may have been fear of punishment. For me, it was fear of overcoming the effects. For both of us, it was facing the judgment of others.

Although the consequences for us may have been different, avoiding them did not make them go away. They continued to grow, seeping into my life, until the task of facing the truth seemed overwhelming—almost impossible.

Emilism: I am afraid, but my courage is stronger.

My brother and I were not the only ones afraid.

I could see panic on my mom's face when I asked her if I could talk to her and my dad privately. A million horrible scenarios must have run through her mind. I wondered if I would be able to find my words. Ryan's presence seemed out of place, but he was there as promised for support.

My mom sat next to me on my bed while my dad stood in the doorway, almost disconnected from the scene. Each of us felt the tension and had the sense our lives were about to change. The truth tumbled out in my own timid way.

I saw my mother's heart shatter. She was devastated. The children she always longed for and had dedicated her life to, were injured in a way she could not fix. She threw her arms around me and sobbed.

Without moving from where he stood, my dad very calmly said, "I will have to ask your brother about this." I don't remember much of the conversation after that, but I do remember tears, sorrow, and wondering what the next day would be like, and the next.

The following week my mom relayed the message that, although it was very difficult for my dad, he had asked and my brother had confirmed it was true. A sense of relief swept over me. I hadn't put any thought into what would happen if he chose to deny it. However, my brother's willingness to acknowledge his actions did not make the situation less complicated.

My life and my family began to crack at the seams, my two little sisters were merely bystanders in the destruction. They were both very young and given minimal information, only enough to determine whether they had been abused. Thankfully they remained innocent, but even in later years as they learned more, neither one of them ever spoke a word of love or concern to me on the subject.

My older sister was the first person I confided in after my parents. After all, I thought she would remember that first night. She seemed to believe the lie about the intruder as much as I did. I shut down when she callously responded, "Well, I'm not going to take sides."

By not picking sides, she picked his.

I don't think this was a conscious decision, but for whatever reason she did not see a clear moral line. Becoming an obstacle in my healing process, I felt as though she was actively against me. When I cried, she accused me of manipulating our family. When I was angry, she suggested it was my responsibility. When I defended myself, I was a liar.

Ryan's assurance of 110% support was anything but. My phone rang and I accepted his invitation to meet for dinner at the local taco shop, but when his front door opened, he clearly had other plans. It was foolish of me to walk over the threshold where we would be alone. Knowing I was in a vulnerable state, he thought I'd go along with his sexual advances, but had enough sense to restrain himself when I said no. The rejection caused him to lash out. "You're damaged. You'll always be damaged." *Was he right?* Possibly.

Our relationship ended and added one more experience to fuel my hatred for men and my feelings of aloneness.

The flood gates opened and unleashed all the feelings I carefully kept hidden away. With no coping skills to fall back on I went with my instincts, which were to promptly begin starving myself. That road had already been paved. I compulsively counted every calorie and snuck into my mom's bathroom multiple times a day to weigh myself. The number on the scale became my obsession as it continued to drop.

The constant feelings of hunger got old fast, and I couldn't maintain my limited diet. I wanted food to comfort me, but I was terrified of gaining weight. So I found another solution.

The clear blue sky was beautiful, as it usually is in southern California, perfect for a small barbecue with friends. I sat in a plastic patio chair and had a staring contest with a blueberry cake covered in whipped frosting. Guilt would come if I ate it, but I was so tired of fighting. The cake won and I went on my first real binge. I couldn't stop eating and no one paid any attention to what was on my plate. When I got home, I took a bottle of water into the bathroom and drank until everything in my stomach came up and out, along with my torment. The only awareness left was a temporary high. I thought I had found the answer. The control I sought took a new form.

Eating consumed my thoughts. It pushed out everything else, which was mainly pain and rejection. Driving home one afternoon, I knew I'd be returning to an empty house. I had two hours before my parents would be home from their meetings. My mind circled through a long list of food items. I could have whatever I wanted because in the end, I would reject it all. It tasted so good and comforting going down. And I will be honest, it felt just as good coming up.

Sometimes when I felt too lazy to throw up, I would go to the grocery store and search the shelves for a box of laxatives. They were purchased with whatever fix I was craving at the time—a bag of cookies there would soon be no trace of. I opened the box of little pills and counted, ten, fifteen, sometimes even twenty and popped them in my mouth. I was like a desperate addict. There were a few times I got seriously sick in the middle of the night, shaking and sweating. It almost wasn't worth it. I promised myself this was the last time. But in the morning when the scale rewarded my efforts, I knew I wouldn't give it up. The cycle would go on and my motivation was refueled.

My head was in a fog, spinning with no direction. In the middle of beauty school now, I spent my breaks throwing up in the bathroom. Students came in and out of the school on a monthly basis, and a graduation was held for each departing group. On that day, a potluck lunch was organized which triggered my worst binge of the month. The back room was filled with cookies, cakes, chips, and all sorts of goodness where I spent most of my day eating away.

Exercise was another obsession.

With every beat of my feet hitting the pavement, I thought about running away from everyone and everything. When the soft music popped on the radio, the alarm clock read 5:00 a.m. I quietly put on my running shoes. My car didn't wake anyone when it started. When I pulled up, the high school track was dimly lit by a few street lights.

I knew there was a homeless man asleep next to the bleachers. I'm sure it was dangerous to be out by myself, but I thought if something happened to me, maybe it would be best for everyone.

My health deteriorated quickly. The number on the scale continued to drop, while my naturally flushed cheeks lost their color. Six months went by without any sign of my menstrual cycle and in some twisted way, it was proof of my own suffocating success.

My mother set up an appointment with a professional LDS counselor. The counselor spent some time affirming the abuse was not my fault. She encouraged me to set boundaries with people in my life that were destructive to my healing, specifically my brother and older sister. When I told my mom she promptly ended my sessions, believing an LDS counselor should never advocate cutting off a family member.

Trying another avenue, my mom took me to speak with my stake president, hoping for some spiritual guidance. Our only conversation consisted mostly of me crying and a handful of kind words spoken by my church leader. His authority did not reach outside of my area, so my admission was passed along to my brother's stake president, and then to his bishop who held the authority to take disciplinary action. When my mom heard my brother and his bishop were surfing buddies, she knew the case would be dropped, and it was.

At some point my dad wrote my brother a letter. He told me of his plan and sat down with me several times to make sure he understood the details of what took place. Although there was much to be considered in regard to the needs of both sides, this was my dad's way of making a stand and saying, "What you did was wrong." Unfortunately, my brother never responded to the letter, and there was never another word spoken. Life was busy, needs were not met, and my dad quickly decided it was time to forgive and move on.

For various reasons, distance had grown between me and any friends I had. I was grasping at someone, anyone, for help when I called a girl I'd been close to in high school. She invited me to the run-down apartment she moved into after being kicked out of her parents' home. Facing her own unfortunate circumstances, she had no sympathy for me. We sat on the curb, shaded by the apartment in the shady downtown neighborhood. She told me to get over myself, that she was the one with real problems. It was the last conversation we ever had.

Counseling was not an option, I was not given any spiritual direction by church leaders, I had no friends, no more discussion with my dad and little with my mom. She made it clear she did not feel comfortable sharing this information with anyone, so I hesitated to speak up. It felt very taboo to talk about, even among the people who should have loved me. I finally revealed this huge secret and everyone treated it as if it was nothing or as though it should remain a secret. Not one single person in my life reached out to help me.

Another sleepless night came, with quiet tears hitting my pillow. I turned to look at the time on my alarm clock and it read 12:13 a.m.—Jess's birthday numbers. It was late and some time had passed since I had connected with my old high school boyfriend, but I grabbed the phone and called his house. The voice on the other line listened while I described my miserable life.

The only reason I turned to Jess was because I was desperate for someone with whom I could feel safe. I never had to censor myself around him. I was being rejected at every turn and knew I could find acceptance with him—although it was a very dysfunctional and selfish kind of acceptance. He took me back into his life with all my baggage, but did not seem to actually care about my mental state. He never encouraged me to seek help, and I am not sure he understood the need for it.

My parents became more concerned about my bulimia and my relationship with Jess, whom they did not like. These things became the focus of our interactions, but they were not the root of my problems. They were cries for help.

By now my dad had moved away for his new job, but I was used to his absence. He and my mom discussed ongoing family events over the phone in the evenings. I'm sure my parents' inability to help me was frustrating for them, but they treated the whole situation like they just wanted it to go away. My mom said many times that she would be okay if I was okay. She didn't want to see me hurt and her attitude put a lot of pressure on me to get past it quickly. My parents were either unwilling or incapable of getting me the help I needed.

Emilism: The sun sheds light on the earth, chasing the shadows away; and the Son sheds light on our hearts, chasing the pains away.

The sexual abuse was horrible, but the sad reality is that the most difficult thing has been the repeated rejection throughout my life, each experience leaving a fresh gaping wound through my heart.

After the truth came out, one family member said we needed to "protect my brother's family." In other words, protect him from the consequences so he would have a chance to move on with his life. Avoidance is *not* protection! Another said, "Everyone does things they regret when they are young." As if this was some childhood folly and I shouldn't make a big deal of it. Abuse is *not* a silly mistake!

These comments and many others that were similar have always confused and bothered me. They left me wondering: *Who will protect me and my family?*

I was ready to start the healing process, but my feelings were swept under the rug and my healing jeopardized for the sake of protecting him. Although I did find healing, the road has been longer and more painful than it needed to be, and I am still isolated from my family in many ways. Hiding from the truth helps no one, not the victim, not the perpetrator, not their families.

Sexual abuse happens in hidden places and hidden hearts, but it's healed in the light: God's light. My decision to let go of my secret altered the entire course of my life, and ultimately put me on the right path. I told the truth. This was a new beginning. Not necessarily a bright one, but one I had to face. I had no clue what to expect. Nothing in my life prepared me for this step.

CHAPTER 4

And behold, I am the light and the life of the world; and I have drunk out of that bitter cup which the Father hath given me, and have glorified the Father in taking upon me the sins of the world, in the which I have suffered the will of the Father in all things from the beginning.
3 Nephi 11:11

Emilism: Let it be okay if people are against you. God will protect your heart.

The subject was broached about whether I should move with my family or remain in California. Since being with them wasn't helping, I decided it would be better for me to be on my own. Everyone probably thought it was a bad idea to leave me behind, but no one pushed for a better solution. I felt like my mom was ready to get rid of me and I think she was afraid to put pressure on me about anything.

After the house sold, my mom packed up and left with my two little sisters. Before they drove away my mom dropped me off with a neighbor who had agreed to take me in.

My new landlords played two faces, spreading rumors about me to my parents and even to the ward in which I grew up. I was hurt when I found out the lady who had been my Young Women Advisor helped spread these lies. It seemed I couldn't catch a break with anyone.

Among the rumors there was a truth: I was having sex. I was so far gone by this point, I honestly thought: *What is the worst thing I can do to myself?* And that was it.

Considering my religious background, it might be surprising to know I never felt guilt over this decision, only regret. Regret that I chose to remove any last shred of virtue that was still mine to keep. I already felt worthless and unclean, and the last little bit I threw away.

Honestly, I don't know what I could have done differently. I was pushed down that path. I had nowhere to turn, emotionally or otherwise, and Jess provided a place to fall.

I purchased a box of eggplant-colored hair dye and used it to cover my wavy blonde locks. My mother loved my hair and would have missed the sun-streaked highlights. I almost cried when I looked in the mirror. The person staring back at me wasn't Emily, but the color reflected my new rebellious personality and the darkness that had taken over my life.

This rebellion led me to more destructive behavior.

I wanted to get in my car, start driving, and never look back. My emotions and the events that took place cannot be put into words. If I stop to reflect on them, I could get lost in my own mind. The memories of this time could swallow me whole.

My bulimia was out of control. I was binging and purging a minimum of three times a day. I was withdrawn and angry. My nonexistent testimony made it so I didn't even believe God would help me. Not that I didn't believe He existed, but I had no way to connect with Him.

I lost my family, friends, and home. Stripped of everything. Left without any kind of guidance. Without God.

Emilism: You must accept life as it comes.

I had very little contact with my parents. They mostly got their information from my crazy landlord. One night I picked up the phone to hear my dad's voice on the other end confronting me about my behavior. He challenged me when I denied it all. "You're a liar." Hearing those words stung, but made me realize I had crossed the line into a place that was so dark even I wasn't sure what the truth was anymore. There was no light left to shed on it. Truth and lies mixed together. It all seemed like a gray mist.

The lying and hiding had depleted my energy. My rebellion was effectively over. I retreated into myself again, passively doing what I was told. It was decided I needed to leave that house. Of all the places, my parents arranged for me to move in with my brother. I think I was there about three weeks. I honestly don't remember one thing during that time. It's just blank in my mind.

I finished beauty school and got my cosmetology license. On graduation day there was no one in the audience for me, but there was plenty of food in the back room where I could binge and purge my emotions away.

My parents bought me a one-way plane ticket out of southern California. I knew where my flight was landing, but I couldn't say the same for my future. The passengers next to me would never know the emotional baggage I carried onto that plane.

I barely talked to my parents during the six weeks I stayed with them. It helped I got my wisdom teeth pulled and my jaw swelled completely shut. But sometimes actions speak louder than words.

One morning I was in a Vicodin-induced haze on my parents' couch. My dad was heading out the door for work. As he went to leave, he turned and came into the living room. He leaned over and kissed me on my forehead, then left. Maybe it was a dream, but I don't think so. This was the first time in my entire life I remember my dad reaching out to show genuine affection towards me. I cherish that moment from him. His kiss seemed to remove a tiny piece of my burden. I knew my parents loved me and they were hurting too.

A light blinked on the answering machine after an evening out. I was surprised when my mom said the message was for me. "Who is it?" Other than a few family members, no one knew where I was. I couldn't imagine who'd be reaching out now. My mom had a soft smile and told me, "Just listen."

The voice I heard was my salvation. "This is Tom. I found this number in an old church directory. I'm looking for Emily."

We spent five hours on the phone that night. At a time when long distance was not free, I think my mom would have paid anything to see me happy.

I *was* happy for those five hours, but Tom and I were passing ships. He returned home from an honorable mission three days after I left California. His place in my heart still existed, but when I said goodbye to California I was at my lowest low—I was not worthy of having him fill it. So when Tom told me he was calling to ask me for a date, there were two obstacles: I was in another state and I said no.

My grandparents moved to Anchorage in 1949, the year the first traffic lights were installed on Fourth Avenue. It was a big deal for my family to travel the long distance to see them, but the time we spent in Alaska was everyone's favorite.

There were family picnics, float trips down the Kenai River, picking raspberries from the bushes in Grandma's garden, and evening card games with the family gathered around the small kitchen table. My favorite activity was to ride bikes on the coastal trail. The trail is ten miles in and ten miles out. It never mattered what time we left, because the sun was up all day and night, making the leaves on the trees glisten as the wind rustled them.

One summer we had a hard time scrounging up enough bikes for everyone so I ended up on a little pink bike with a banana seat. I rode the whole twenty miles on that bike with no gears or hand brakes, but I loved every minute of it.

My older sister ended up engaged to a young man she met during one of these family trips. There was plenty of downtime for me while others ran around placing orders and setting appointments for the wedding. I was happy to be in Alaska and in my grandparents' home where I felt safe, but there were still no real discussions about how to recover from the damage done. In an effort to keep my mind occupied, my mom put me to work sewing a quilt and I settled down.

My grandma's sewing room was always neat and tidy. Every color of thread hung on the rack my grandpa had lovingly constructed for her in his workshop. I watched the needle on my grandma's sewing machine pulse up and down while the pattern of white squares and appliqué hearts came together with each row.

I'm not pulled away from a project easily, so I can't explain the impulse I felt to walk down the green carpeted steps into my grandparents' basement. I was drawn to the door in the far corner where I could hear voices. I stood quietly on the other side listening to my mother's conversation with my sister and her fiancé. They were talking about me! I felt a rush of anger at the thought of the three of them discussing my life, and not a single one of them willing to have that conversation with me. I pushed the door open and screamed. Hysterics took over and I ran back up the staircase with my mom a few steps behind me. She grabbed me and I fell down in her lap sobbing for I don't know how long.

That night she and I took a drive down the windy road that led to the inlet. The sun hung on the horizon, creating the dusky Alaskan sky. A good cry brought some release, but the real conversation still did not happen. Instead, my thoughts turned to Tom.

When I called him the next day he was excited to hear from me and glad to know I had changed my mind about a date. He'd already booked a ticket to Utah, where my parents made plans to send me. I wasn't sure where my life was headed, but I had no issue with moving there, and everyone hoped this would give me a fresh start.

Tom and I planned for me to pick him up from the airport. When the day finally came, I was filled with anticipation. Deep down I knew he was the one—he had always been the one.

When the crowd of passengers began filing out the gate, I could feel my cheeks turning the same shade of pink as the shirt I wore. I sat in a chair and put my cold hands over my face trying to reduce the flush of color. While the crowd continued to pass by, I began to panic. *It's been so long. Will I recognize him?*

My entire future walked my way. I stood up and Tom put his arms around me. I did recognize him and I recognized his embrace from when we danced together years before.

During the first days we were reunited, Tom heard my whole painful story. He gave me what no one else had, complete acceptance. "Everything is going to be okay. I will make you happy." His faith in me was unshaken. Tom loved me so much and I loved him. He was different than any other man. I thought I might be able to ride out the rest of my life on his strength. I believed his love would save me and he believed the same.

A diamond ring was on my left hand and a temple marriage was our goal. Hoping to relieve myself from the past and be worthy for the future, I confided in my bishop. At first it was just to confess my sins, but at his questioning I also disclosed the abuse. His countenance was kind. He saw my intentions were true. He was going to seek guidance on my behalf and meet with me again in a few weeks. His conclusion was that no disciplinary action should be taken. "And Jesus said unto her, Neither do I condemn thee: go, and sin no more" (John 8:11).

Six months later Tom and I were sitting, just the two of us, in the celestial room of the San Diego California Temple. In all my life, this is my most treasured memory. Our friends and family were waiting for us in the sealing room, but for that moment we were only focused on each other. The sun lit on Tom's face through the blue stained glass, bringing out his freckles. I knew he was made for me, that God intended us to be together, that Tom promised to take care of me and I promised to help him get to heaven.

His love gave me a safe place, but Tom's love alone could not save me. Over time we both suffered when faced with this reality.

I found myself back in California to be with Tom, but the move was not good for me. California is full of painful memories, and I still feel like I regress a little when I go back there.

Four months into our marriage, Tom and I accepted my grandparents' offer to live in their basement rent-free. We packed our Volkswagen Jetta with what little we owned and drove four thousand miles up the west coast and through Canada to make a new start in Anchorage, Alaska. The love of my life sat two feet away from me in the driver's seat. I knew it was hard for him to leave his family and friends behind. His sacrifice was made for my rescue, and I loved him even more for it.

I got my first real taste of freedom watching the scenery change with each passing mile. God must have taken extra care when he created this part of the world. The crisp air has a unique clean forest scent. The towering mountains reach well above the tree line, making the city seem miniature. In the winter snow blows across the road matching the long wispy patterns of the northern lights. The landscape was completely opposite from the tumbleweeds and palm trees I left behind.

Maybe it was just an escape, but Alaska drew me in. It became a place of safety and refuge, a home where my heart belongs.

Emilism: You push people away and cause your own loneliness.

I was happy to be in Alaska and I loved Tom more than anything, but I was still just going through the motions of life. I made covenants in the temple. I went to church and held callings, but still did not have a real testimony. When I think back on that time, I was very childlike, as if I were still twelve years old pretending to be an adult.

The pressures of what transpired over the previous two years took a toll on my relationships with my parents and siblings. They never supported me and did not understand me. They seemed more neutral than anything else. I know my parents didn't like what my brother did, but they were not willing to go the distance with me.

Sometimes people refer to hell as the inability to progress while knowing you could have done better, a kind of personal hell. Abuse is hell! When sexual abuse occurs, it creates a state of unrest where there is an inability to progress or find peace. The disconnect between the problem and the solution creates what I think of as a gap. Ultimately this state of unrest, this gap, is caused by an inability to trust. It is magnified in victims of sexual abuse because the victims' boundaries have been broken in such a profound way, most often by someone they trusted.

Woven throughout my soul was an incomplete maze, full of dead ends. There never seemed to be an answer or a way out. My gaps destroyed any sense of identity. I knew I was different from other people. My internal dialogue was in constant turmoil. *How much of this experience defines me? How do I move forward without it? How do I recognize my authentic self? When and whom should I share this with and how much? Can people really know who I am without knowing this part of me? What things are normal struggles and what are directly caused by the abuse? I want to heal, but I am not sure if I can or if I want to let go of my pain. I want to live a happy life, but I keep finding myself revisiting these emotions. I want people to love me, but they never say the right thing.*

I was suspicious of everyone in my life, which affected all my relationships even the closest ones. I waited with a sharp eye for anything that could possibly hurt me. I didn't believe I could get approval from my family, questioned the loyalty of my friends, and withheld information from my husband for no apparent reason. I would not put forth the effort to move my emotional growth forward because I did not believe healing could happen for me.

This is not to say I was unjustified in my state of mind. Everything about my experience taught me I could trust nothing and no one. Sadly for me, trust is a requirement for healing and one of the most difficult things to be repaired once broken.

CHAPTER 5

What man of you, having an hundred sheep, if he lose one of
them, doth not leave the ninety and nine in the wilderness,
and go after that which is lost, until he find it?
Luke 15:4

Emilism: We are all "The One" to some degree during
times we feel forsaken in our trials. Even people who
appear happy can be lost in their hearts.

Tom and I were married for a year and a half when I
discovered I was pregnant. Excitement took over. I was
convinced the baby would be a little girl. I even picked out a
name and bought pink clothes. When the doctor moved the
ultrasound over my round belly she announced, "It's a boy!" In
an instant my excitement was replaced with overwhelming
sadness.

I turned my head away from the picture and a tear dripped
down my cheek. I wasn't supposed to have boys. Sure, I would
be okay with having the token son after I had a few girls, but I

never imagined those girls having a big brother. *How could God do this to me? I could not love a boy. Tom was the exception.* I fell into a depression and cried for three days. My mood finally shifted when I opened a package from my mom and pulled out some little blue overalls.

My son was born a few months later. He was the most beautiful thing I'd ever seen. I did love him, with a deep and abiding love that I had never felt before—a mother's love. I had a little miracle. Being a mother sparked something deep inside me. I would do anything to protect my child. I would do whatever it took to create the best possible life for him. I would break every bad habit and unhealthy cycle so he could grow up feeling safe and loved.

For the first time in my life I made the long walk to the front of the chapel to bear my testimony. I'm not sure what I said. The decision was motivated more by the birth of my first child than a true belief. Nevertheless, attending to my own spirituality was a way to keep the promise I made to my infant. Being active in the church my entire life, even going to the temple, had never given me the desire to read the scriptures. And so as a mother, I picked up the Book of Mormon for the first time and began to read. "And oh, what joy, and what marvelous light I did behold; yea, my soul was filled with joy as exceeding as was my pain!" (Alma 36:20).

My previous attempts at reading scripture always left me confused. This time was different. With my little bundle of blue next to me, I had motivation. I searched the pages with an honest heart. When I read the account of Alma's redemption his testimony filled me with hope. These prophetic words stuck with me and I began to believe the same could happen to me. Maybe there was some joy for me. If my joy could be as exceeding as all the pain I continued to live with, then I had a great deal of joy in store.

Scribbling notes on sheets of loose paper was enlightening. I drew connections in the storyline and was inspired by scriptural examples of faith. I finally knew what everyone else at church knew, the Book of Mormon is true. My first living testimony. I was quite proud of myself for this little step.

Gaining this piece of knowledge led me to believe all was well. Now at a plateau I was able to maintain through self-reliance, I decided the past would resolve itself. I played the part of active mother and loving wife, doing all the checklist things. The problem was, instead of healing, I was becoming a hardcore perfectionist. I thought I needed to prove to God I was worth something for Him to love me. I didn't realize, He already did.

I can't imagine what people thought of me during those years. I must have come across so scattered. I was terrible at relationships, so insecure, yet tried desperately to keep up the appearance of being mature and having my life together. On the inside I wanted to scream. Sometimes I went months without sleeping. Lying in bed for hours, my mind twisted and turned. Couldn't anyone see how much I was still suffering? I was looking more for someone to share my burdens than for true friendship. But I could have spread my burdens out over a thousand people and it still would not have been enough.

My poor Tom. He was so incredibly patient. There could not have been a more loving and true man. He provided a safe place and gave me all the love he had, but I disappointed him. He needed my love as well, and I had none to give. When he realized his love wasn't enough to fix my broken heart it created a wedge between us.

Emilism: Love is not a contest

The gap in my marriage was widening, I couldn't connect with people, and couldn't build a true relationship with God. Even though I still didn't understand the gaps that were growing, they left a void in their wake, which I tried to fill with whatever I could. Lacking the correct tools or perspective, these behaviors were compulsive not intentional. One of these things was bulimia, which still lingered off and on. However, most of the fillers were wholesome activities, or so I thought.

I never gave up playing the piano. After I got married, I put myself in lessons with a strict Russian woman. "Not so close. Sit up straight. Wrists down. Fingers curled. Move the weight in your arm with the keys," she would chide. I thought by perfecting this art I could set myself apart as an accomplished musician. When I played, it was never for myself, but for others to admire me.

Everything I set out to accomplish was done to perfection.

I needed to be the best cook and if I brought a dish to any function, it was always the most beautiful. I had a reputation to keep up, so at Christmastime I made elaborate truffle trees and candies. When I had people over for dinner I never thought about the cost, only the presentation.

My space was always clean and I always looked my best. I found many external things to obsess over. Life was like a never-ending checklist of tasks to be done. I did not find joy in these things, but if I could check everything off the list, perfection might be achieved.

I have a very detailed eye and buried myself in projects like quilting and crocheting. I was drawn to these types of things because, much like my bulimia, I could let them consume my thoughts with counting loops, lining up blocks, and perfecting patterns. Focusing on these projects helped push away other feelings like anxiety, which I still struggled with.

In every position at church I worked on my own idea of perfection producing cute handouts, cards, and gifts. I see now how opportunities for spiritual growth were overlooked, but every other detail was thought out as I, in a sense, packaged my life.

People knew me for these "talents", so my fillers provided some attention. I tried to find an identity this way, controlling how people saw me. But what I portrayed was something I could never be—perfect. I set myself up for failure because the things on my checklist grew faster than I could check them off. When, inevitably I could not keep up, my feelings of failure only increased my loneliness. My cries for help could never be heard when they were suffocated under my perfectionist personality.

How badly I wanted and needed to be loved. And even though Tom tried to provide this love, nothing seemed to fill that gap, which was the largest of all. Sadly for me, love is another requirement for healing.

Emilism: Only the Atonement justifies your life.

Tom approached me with a heavy heart. A family member had given birth and the police were at her apartment to take custody of the baby girl. The father was an accused child molester. At first opening my home to this child seemed like a wild idea, but the more I thought about it the more it made sense. My trials had prepared me to protect and nurture her. I thought saving someone else from what I had gone through would justify my life or make sense of my suffering. But I was approaching it the same way Tom did with me. Tom thought he could save me, and I thought I could save this innocent little girl. By doing so I would be a hero, which would finally fill the gap in my entire existence. It was almost like saving myself.

I put all my effort and hope into making my home ready for her arrival. When the plan unraveled, I was heartbroken and empty. The thing I thought would justify my life was not to be.

One of my mistakes during this time, and for a long time afterward, was focusing my decisions on proving myself to others and to God, whom I did not know, that I was worth loving. I did not know, understand, or feel love so I mistook it for the approval of others.

It took me years to realize these fillers could not justify my life. They could not fill the gaps or prove me worthy of being loved. Healing must come from within. It does not come from outside influences or the approval of others. Until the Atonement takes effect, true love will never be known. This is what each person who comes to this earth needs to discover.

My discovery was still to come.

Emilism: Not everything happens for a reason.

Up to this point, I spent most of my life living in the dark. I tried to find stability in these fillers. I felt like I was spinning my wheels, giving so much, and yet frustrated I was going nowhere. I spent a lot of time pondering the mistakes I made, the paths I had taken, and wondered if I was lost or just a lost cause. "Some [are lost] because they are different, some because they are weary, and some because they have strayed" (Joseph B. Worthlin [1]).

I was lost because I felt different and weary. Other than my husband, who was also growing weary, I had nowhere to turn. I carried a lot of guilt about the past and about not being able to move forward. I never missed a week of church in my life, yet I spent all these years, and many to come, feeling lost and alone. I was "The One", the lost sheep left wandering without its shepherd.

One summer Sunday I sat in a pew listening to prelude music when the bishop of my ward approached me. "Would you be willing to offer our closing prayer?" I burst into tears. He understood my reaction to mean "No", apologized for asking, and assured me he would find someone else. The thought of coming out of my protective shell terrified me. Feelings of inadequacy caused me to believe I would never measure up to the impossible expectation I had set for a true disciple of Christ.

Sunday School was always a scary venture. I listened intently to the teacher and the comments made by others, but their testimonies were out of my reach. I felt like I was falling behind while everyone else was speeding ahead.

At times I found the preaching hypocritical. It didn't seem to provide a framework for my experiences. Inside I cringed every time I heard the comment, "Everything happens for a reason," or "God will never give you any trials you cannot handle." I wondered why God hadn't protected me or stopped the abuse.

I was expected to handle my own trials, but I felt bitter. The Christlike love so readily encouraged at church had never been extended to me. I wanted to blame the people whose choices caused my heartache, from my family for not supporting me down to my visiting teachers who never showed up. If I looked, I could always find someone to blame for holding me back from being happy.

I felt guilt for some of the trials I brought on myself. Whether that guilt was deserved or not, I put myself down every time I failed to achieve the perfection I sought. Other trials I faced came for a variety of reasons. Most of the reasons were unexplainable. They were a result of this imperfect world, but I did not want my suffering to be in vain.

Years later I read the words of Paul in 1 Corinthians 13:7. "Beareth all things, believeth all things, hopeth all things, endureth all things." I was filled with hope and courage that I might be able to endure to the end. This insight came to my mind: *If you did not have the gospel in your life, then you would be truly lost. It has given you hope in ways that you sometimes could not see.*

I didn't know it at the time, but the gospel of Jesus Christ was what kept me moving forward.

CHAPTER 6

*Often the deep valleys of our present will be understood only
by looking back on them from the mountains of our future
experience. Often we can't see the Lord's hand in our lives
until long after trials have passed. Often the most difficult
times of our lives are essential building blocks that form the
foundations of our character and pave the way to future
opportunity, understanding, and happiness.*
Dieter F. Uchtdorf (2)

Emilism: Do not be weary. In the Lord's time, the light
will come. If you have faith the Lord will not fail.

Tom and I had our second child, my little girl. Shortly after
we moved to Missoula, Montana for Tom's schooling. He went
down four weeks ahead of me to obtain an apartment in
student housing.

It was hard to leave Alaska, but we decided it was time to
commit to a full-time school schedule in order to secure our
future. The move lowered our cost of living so we could afford

this goal. Before these plans were put into motion, Tom and I knelt by the side of our bed and prayed for guidance. Unfamiliar with answered prayers, I wondered at being filled with a new confidence I had not experienced before.

My first impression of Missoula was that it was like a smaller version of Alaska. The mountains were not so grand, the wilderness not so rugged, but the overall feel was similar. The people there like a rural lifestyle, and it reminded me enough of home I thought I could make it work.

When I walked in the front door of our run-down student apartment; however, I immediately felt a knot in the pit of my stomach. I couldn't put my finger on it, but I knew something was not right. I thought it was the decor. The metal cabinets, red cement floors, and windows placed at an unusual six feet from the floor. It felt more like a prison than a place for my family to live.

With Tom attending classes for the day, I was still getting used to my new surroundings. I flipped on the computer and logged onto the internet. Moving the cursor over the history icon I clicked. Pornography littered the history log. The knot in my stomach moved into my throat. I felt sick.

Shaking, I picked up the phone and dialed Tom's number. Trying to keep a calm voice, I told him about my findings. He pretended to be surprised. "It must have been my brother," who had helped him move. I wanted to believe his denials. It was easier when the truth meant facing yet another crippling betrayal by someone who should love me.

I was inside, unaware, while Tom paced back and forth in the walkway of our apartment building. Twenty minutes slowly ticked by as he contemplated how his future would change in an instant. He planned to tell me the truth, but couldn't do it over the phone. He knew his confession would destroy me. Although it wasn't working, as shown in this new trial, Tom was the only person I leaned on. Before myself, before family or friends, before God, there was Tom and then only fillers.

He took my hand and sat me down on the couch, but wouldn't look me in the eye. His truth came out along with more than twenty years of my own untouched baggage. I lost all sense of control. I allowed myself to break down, as low as I wanted to go. "I hate you. How could you do this to me?" Once again, I was alone in the world. A black hole opened, sucking away all the stability I thought I had built—it was endless.

I took the only picture of Christ we had in our apartment. Frustrated and angry thinking *He* was never there for me, I smashed the picture against the side of my piano. The glass shattered and pieces flew across the floor. But as soon as the picture hit the ground I regretted the impulsive decision.

At the end of my breakdown I turned to my two little babies who had witnessed the scene and did what any mother would do. I knelt down to soothe them. "It's going to be okay," I told my son and picked up the baby. I sat on the couch with my daughter. She had but few needs in her world. I opened my shirt to nurse her. Suddenly I was startled by a police officer standing in front of me, not even aware he had entered the apartment.

Two policemen responded to a call made by our neighbors who heard me yelling. The other officer sat with Tom in the walkway outside. Humiliated and exhausted, I sat there powerless, my exposed chest like my over-exposed life, and shards of glass covering the floor like my broken heart, impossible to put back together.

✳ ✳ ✳

The decision to partake in pornography was out of character for Tom. He is a protector by nature and his one true wish in life is to love and provide for a wife and children. There are many things in Tom's past that led him to turn to this emotional escape. But his actions could also be considered yet another devastating effect of the abuse I suffered and how it rippled throughout my life.

At twelve years of age Tom did something unusual for a boy so young. He knelt down and dedicated himself to his future wife, promising God he would remain pure. He kept his promise, treating every girl he dated with respect, understanding that she was someone's future wife. Unfortunately, his future wife (me) was broken, cutting him off from love and emotional intimacy. I couldn't find peace and happiness, which made it difficult for Tom to feel like he was providing for the family he always wanted. His goals for school and a career were also not being realized. Nothing seemed to be going as planned. Pornography did for him what bulimia did for me—it was a mask of the true pains in his life, overwhelming feelings of failure. The large gaps in my life caused me to misunderstand the root of this problem and I took it as a personal betrayal, breaking my faith and trust in him. The person whom I thought would be my salvation I had unknowingly pushed to the edge.

In our individual suffering, Tom and I grew farther apart. He withdrew and there was a quiet passiveness to him I had never seen before. Even though he chose to seek help from church leaders a few months later there were more pornographic pictures on our computer.

Upon finding the new evidence I ripped open our closet door and grabbed a suitcase. Tom's face looked broken when I told him I was leaving, but sadly, I had nowhere to go. Instead, I found some comfort relieving my stress over the toilet. Thoughts of killing myself returned, but I could never do that to the people in my life, no matter how strained those relationships were. So I pressed forward, never giving voice to those feelings.

One afternoon I buckled the baby into her pink umbrella stroller and zipped my son's sweater. When I left my apartment the only sign of the coming winter was the yellow color on the falling leaves. We had walked four blocks in the sunshine to an appointment, but now it was getting misty outside. We wouldn't mind a little moisture on our walk back. But when I stepped outside the mist had already turned into large raindrops. There was only one way to get home so I stepped out from under the covered walkway with my children. One block and the rain turned into small pieces of hail, another block and it was flakes of snow. By the time we reached our apartment building, clusters of snowflakes as large as quarters were falling. The melting flakes dripped down my back. The three of us were soaking wet. The shelter of our apartment building was only a few feet away now, but I stopped and took a minute to consider the irony. Even Mother Nature was against me. And she must have had a good laugh because as soon as we were inside the clouds dispersed and the sun took over the sky once again.

Tom and I both faced so many disappointments in Montana. I felt like an outcast in our ward with our problems on display. At the closing of a Sunday School lesson the teacher asked Tom to offer the prayer. As part of the repentance process he had agreed to restrict his church privileges for a time. He quietly responded, "I can't." But the teacher did not hear and asked again for a prayer. Louder this time for all to witness, Tom responded, "I can't say the prayer."

The shadow of darkness created a constant feeling of heaviness in my chest, making it difficult to breath. Life's challenges were piling up and I couldn't see any way out. Time slowly rolled to a standstill. I decided I had two options, either end it all or make a last-ditch effort to lay it out for God.

My feet felt heavy as they dragged me into my small bedroom. With a sigh my knees hit the ground and I put my head against the soft comforter. "Heavenly Father ... please help me ...," then nothing. No words would form, my mind was blank. There seemed to be no words to express what I felt, there was only sorrow. "ANYTHING ... please ..." I didn't know what I needed. I didn't understand how lost I was until I stepped into the light.

CHAPTER 7

"If ye have faith as a grain of mustard seed, ye shall say unto this mountain, Remove hence to yonder place; and it shall remove" (Matt. 17:20). I have never witnessed the removal of an actual mountain. But because of faith I have seen a mountain of doubt and despair removed and replaced with hope and optimism. Because of faith I have personally witnessed a mountain of sin replaced with repentance and forgiveness. And because of faith I have personally witnessed a mountain of pain replaced with peace, hope, and gratitude. Yes, I have seen mountains removed.
Richard C. Edgley (3)

Emilism: Don't ask why me!

The church cleared out after an evening women's activity, but I stayed behind and slid onto the bench of the chestnut-stained piano. I flipped open the hymnal and discovered a prayer of hope on page 99. Someone who lived long before my time wrote the words I had been searching for. I played the notes for the first time and sang the words that spoke to me of the depth of my trials, the painful refining, and my hope of rescue.

> *Nearer, dear Savior, to thee, nearer, nearer to thee—*
> *Ever I'm striving to be nearer, yet nearer to thee!*
> *Trusting, in thee I confide; hoping, in thee I abide.*
> *Proved by my trials, I'll be nearer, yet nearer to thee!*
> *Humbly I come to thee now; earnest, I prayerfully bow.*
> *Ever my anthem will be nearer, yet nearer to thee!*
> *Loving thee, ever I pray, aid me thy will to obey.*
> *Let me by holiness be nearer, yet nearer to thee!*
> *When all my trials are done, when my reward I have won,*
> *Take, oh, take, and cherish me,*
> *Nearer, dear Savior, to thee!*

This hymn inspired me to write my own prayer, not one set to music, but to the commotion of life. The kids and I took weekly trips to the mall. My daughter is an animal lover so we spent time in the pet store, and then in the play area where my son jumped around on the child-size train. Sitting in the middle of the bustle, I dug through my bag for a sheet of paper and a pen, and began writing:

Dear Heavenly Father,

The things I carry are so heavy. It makes life so hard sometimes. I feel so unworthy and so unloved. I question my abilities and whether I am a good mother and a good wife. I try to have faith, but it is so hard because

I have never had much to hold onto. Is life like this for everyone? Am I doing something wrong? I am not going to ask why me. Does it really matter why? I just know that I am what I am. I do sometimes wonder how I would have been different if certain things hadn't happened. I have struggled with my testimony a lot. I have lost so much faith in myself, and the people around me. I sometimes think I know what the answer is, but I get confused about what is right. It is hard for me to sift through it all. I know that I try and maybe, little by little, things are getting better, but it is so hard for me to hear if I am doing something wrong. I get so down and beat myself up that I feel like I don't have one more ounce of energy to put into making this better. I am not sure if my faith is strong enough to get the help I need from you and to be able to fix the things that are broken.

—Help me to choose to be happy.

—Give me strength.

—Help me to understand the purpose of my life.

—Give me faith.

—Help me forgive.

—Don't let me put so much into what people say.

—Help me be more understanding and give people the benefit of the doubt.

—Help me like myself.

—I want to feel the Spirit and know that you will help me.

—I don't want to be confused anymore.

—I can't be perfect, but I am doing the best I can. What will qualify me?

—What am I supposed to do with my feelings?

—Help me find security in my unstable world.

—Help the time to go by fast and keep my eyes on the goal.

—Help me to see the blessings.

—What am I worth?

—I need someone to love me.

—Make it easier for me to be around people.

My mind is slowing down and I am running out of things to say. I am begging you to help me fix this. Help me know where to find help and what steps to take. Please forgive me for my weakness.

Love,

Emily

I reviewed my list—all the things I needed. I folded the paper, tucked it safely away in my bag, and left the mall with kids in tow.

After the kids were quietly napping in their rooms, I returned to the side of my bed. I unfolded my letter. With all the heart I could summon I made another attempt to pray. This time I had the words written down. As I read aloud the items on my list, I turned each one over to God admitting I was spent. I didn't have the answers and I couldn't change the past. I was powerless to stop the pain. Through my sobbing I begged Him to fix me.

My tower of burdens reached a breaking point, driving me full force towards the gospel. Apparently, some of the things I had been taught stuck. I was in no way a gospel scholar, but I quickly learned how to connect with God in a most sincere and powerful way—through honest prayer.

I began using my journals as a source of communication with God. As I recorded my deepest thoughts, I imagined the picture of Christ, by Del Parson, in a red robe knocking at the door with no handle. "Behold, I stand at the door, and knock: if any man hear my voice, and open the door, I will come in to him" (Revelation 3:20). Opening an actual door is a simple task, but the true meaning behind the picture, opening one's heart, takes time and preparation. I was brought to a place where opening that door was my best option, but all I could do was stand in front of it. My heart was tightly shut.

I often went running before Tom left to attend his classes. My headphones were blaring in my ears one sunny morning, but I tuned it out. My mind was in another place, searching, wondering, pondering God and His role in my life. I looked up at the blue sky. There were only a few wispy clouds. I tried to imagine how far the heavens stretched. *Where was God? Was He looking down on me?* I silently begged: *HELP ME!*

A warm feeling filled my entire body, rushing through my heart, and bringing with it these words, "God loves you; He sees you, and you are unique." They were not my own words, but they were words spoken to me from some familiar place— a place I recognized as truth.

This was the first time I truly felt God's love along with the warmth and peace it brought. I began to crave that love. However, this experience was like throwing a starving man a loaf of bread. It tastes amazing and fills him for a time, but when it's gone, he is only left begging for more.

Over time doubts clouded my memory of this moment, and I often thought the light at the end of the tunnel was a train bearing down on me. I questioned everything, wondering if I was spending my last reserves hoping for some unseen rescue. This was the only time in my life I seriously considered leaving the church—it seemed too easy to give up on everything I had been taught.

I was asked to play the piano for a baptism. I wanted to say no because I really wasn't in a mood for giving out favors, but I said yes anyway. I played the opening song and then sat alone and felt alone, lost in the crowd.

A little eight-year-old girl entered the water and took her father's hand. She was so innocent, so happy for this day. The warm feeling came back and entered my heart in the same way it had before. The familiar words spoke again, "What she is doing is right and you know it." I looked up at a picture of Christ on the wall, His gentle eyes pierced mine.

Emilism: Do not let your judgment be clouded. Reach out to God, feel of His love, and receive peace.

Two years had passed from my arrival in Montana. Tom was a few classes away from finishing his bachelor's degree, but didn't get accepted to the professional program he applied for. We'd had enough of Missoula and he could finish those classes online, so there was nothing more to keep us there.

The time was not a waste though. We had learned some difficult lessons. Tom walked through the steps of repentance, and I was opening up to my own truths. Together we set healthy boundaries for the computer and no more pornographic pictures appeared in our home. Finally realizing Tom's love couldn't save me, we both took a hard look at our relationship. We were farther apart than ever, but were more committed than ever to building a brighter future.

We decided to go back to Anchorage, but planning our move felt like walking through thick mud—slow and frustrating. There was a tangible dark presence in our lives. Elder Jeffrey R. Holland's words are descriptive of our attempts, "If sometimes the harder you try, the harder it gets, take heart. So it has been with the best people who ever lived" (4). This move was our last push, our chance to put the past behind us and move forward reunited.

Tom ended up driving with our son back to Anchorage while my daughter and I flew. As our plane sped up and lifted off the ground, defying the laws of gravity, I felt the same kind of weight lifting off me. Knowing the next time I touched ground would be in Alaska was liberating.

My desperate prayers were finally answered when I landed in Anchorage. As I drove away from the airport toward the city that was home to my heart a strange feeling swept over me. It was as if I had never been gone, as though the past two years in Missoula never happened. The pain experienced there seemed to melt away. And not only the pain experienced in Missoula, but the adversity throughout my life. It was all behind me and none of it mattered anymore. I was home.

This is what it must feel like to die.

I imagined crossing into heaven and realizing I was back in the place where I belonged with my Father in Heaven—the place that is home to my spirit. In His presence, none of the challenges of this life will matter. The hardships and weaknesses will all be behind me, and the only thing that will remain will be the person I have become.

With that thought all those challenges that had piled up, brick by oppressive brick building a wall of tribulation, came tumbling down in one powerful blow. The dark shadow cast all those years ago, vanished. Before me was light and hope. It filled my soul. I'd never felt anything like it before. Hell was over. For the first time, I could take a deep breath. The air that filled my lungs felt rich. I remember an amazing feeling of freedom, comfort, and release. This was no small morsel thrown at a starving soul, this moment ended the hunger.

The strange thing about this memory is that I landed in Anchorage in the middle of the night; it was completely dark outside. Yet I remember the sun shining bright and not a cloud in the sky.

Tom and I settled into an apartment in south Anchorage with our two small children. Soon after, I asked him to give me a priesthood blessing. In our room dimly lit by the evening sun, he placed his hands on my head. Carrying a gift of peace and light, the Holy Spirit brought words of truth. I knew a restoration was taking place in my heart, but did not fully understand it. I was taken aback when Tom uttered the words, "Your virtue has been restored."

Emilism: The Adversary has had a lot of control over your life until now. You can close the door on him and open the door to God.

I've always had a fear of open water, which is strange considering my years as a swimmer. I think what scares me about open water is the vastness of what lies beneath.

One night my dreams placed me in the ocean surrounded by dark, rocky water. I could see land far away, but finding myself all alone, I was overwhelmed and panicked. Digging deep for courage, I pushed through my fear and began swimming as fast as I could.

After reaching the soft sand I sat with my feet pointed towards the waves. I looked out over the wide ocean and the distance I swam. The sun shone down on me and I heard God's voice as if it were coming from heaven through those warm rays. He told me a whale had been swimming under me in the dark water. It would have swallowed me, but He had tied it down so I could make it to the safety of the shore.

Looking back on my life with greater understanding, I can see how many times God protected me. I certainly did not feel it at the time. When I was swimming in the ocean I felt all alone and so scared. I was facing my biggest fears. I had no idea God watched over me from above and protected me from beneath.

CHAPTER 8

For he is the same yesterday, today, and forever; and the way is prepared for all men from the foundation of the world, if it so be that they repent and come unto him. For he that diligently seecatch shall find; and the mysteries of God shall be unfolded unto them, by the power of the Holy Ghost, as well in these times as in times of old, and as well in times of old as in times to come; wherefore, the course of the Lord is one eternal round.
1 Nephi 10:18-19

Emilism: Sunday School answers—answer prayers.

I did it! I shed the darkness and stepped into the light. In that transforming moment, driving towards Anchorage, I knew God loved me unconditionally. In spite of all the things wrong with my life He "reached my reaching" (Hymn #129) and pulled me from the depths. I no longer had to prove myself to God; He proved Himself to me. My life that had been void of love was now filled with God's love. This was where I began to learn to love. I realized that no matter the depths He would come for me.

My healing process wasn't complete, but I began to put my trust in Him. He showed me His love at the perfect moment for it to have the greatest healing effect. The words of my Russian piano teacher rang true. "Timing is everything. Without timing, there is no song."

Shedding the darkness was a huge step forward, but there was still so much I did not understand about God, His love that provided this healing, or the patterns that cause this infinite love to ebb and flow drawing me even closer to Him. However, I did understand that it came and embraced my life.

I had the smallest flicker of faith that help would come, and help did come through God's tender mercies. My dream of swimming to shore, the love sent during my morning run in response to a pleading heart, an answer given to relieve my doubts, and a hymn discovered to guide my prayers. The moments when God's love reached through the darkness to uplift my troubled soul, these were tender mercies. "But behold, I, Nephi, will show unto you that the tender mercies of the Lord are over all those whom he hath chosen, because of their faith, to make them mighty even unto the power of deliverance" (1 Nephi 1:20).

Although in desperation I did everything I could to reach out to Him, ultimately mercy was the only explanation for these moments of peace. These were moments I often went back to during times I stumbled in the dark. By remembering how I felt I could draw a little bit of light. Now these are the cornerstones of my testimony of the gospel of Jesus Christ.

I reached *a destination*. I left the dark tunnel behind to walk in the light of God's love. I learned God's love is never changing and ever-constant, a hard concept to understand in a world that is constantly changing. The feelings of light and hope never went away, but healing is a journey, not a destination.

Emilism: Father in Heaven did not design suffering. It is not your destiny to be beaten down. It is your destiny to become Christlike and live with God again.

I had my whole life ahead of me. God's grace put me on the right path, but I'd only made my first few steps. The path ahead still needed to be paved. Even so, that could wait. For the time being I enjoyed a season of peace.

I continued my church attendance in a new ward. I found a seat on one of the green padded chairs lined up for the third hour. The lesson that day was on the purpose of trials. I could welcome hearing about a heart-wrenching trial, but I grew concerned when the comments turned to tears and questions about life's injustices.

A woman who I admired greatly sat in front of me. She was a beautiful woman with a beautiful testimony. The spiritual reserve she had built lifted the people around her, offering a great source of strength. Her hand rose and she admitted she felt her life had been too easy. She expressed guilt for not having to pass through some major trial as if the absence of suffering meant her strength had not been proven. Her admission brought a rush of sadness over me.

The following week we met by chance in the coat room of the temple. I reminded her of the comment she made and told her in a few short sentences of the suffering I endured. I told her how I felt about her. Mostly I wanted to tell her I didn't think someone had to suffer some great tragedy to be a good person. Tears formed in her eyes as she said thank you. The next words she spoke remain with me still. "There is no virtue in suffering."

Trials will be part of this mortal experience, but suffering is not proof of strength. True character comes from the strength it takes to dedicate oneself to God. He allowed me to suffer until I realized my salvation was only through Him. My trials stripped me of everything, and then in His time God took my empty shell and filled it with His pure love.

When I sat in that Sunday lesson on trials, instead of wondering why God had not protected me from the abuse I felt humbled by the pure knowledge that He had saved me. Not just from the abuse, but from all my sins and afflictions, a stark contrast from the attitude I previously held.

> *But that ye would humble yourselves before the Lord, and call on his holy name, and watch and pray continually, that ye may not be tempted above that which ye can bear, and thus be led by the Holy Spirit, becoming humble, meek, submissive, patient, full of love and all long-suffering; Having faith on the Lord; having a hope that ye shall receive eternal life; having the love of God always in your hearts, that ye may be lifted up at the last day and enter into his rest.*
> *Alma 13:28-29*

This scripture helped me understand that sentiments such as "Everything happens for a reason" and "God will not give you any trials you cannot handle" carry some truth, but are only applicable when relying upon the Lord for one's welfare.

As the lesson came to a close the teacher said through her tears, "I don't know what the answer is. I don't know why bad things happen." But I did know why. "[T]hou knowest the greatness of God; and he shall consecrate thine afflictions for thy gain" (2 Nephi 2:2).

Although consecration is a process involving many correct choices, in my moment of healing it was a single choice to completely dedicate myself to the God who saved me. With this vow my heart was turned, and the only reason left for all those years of suffering was to purify my life.

Tom placed his hands upon my head again. This time his words brought closure, answering my heart's desire to know why these things happened to me. "You should not have had to experience some of the things you have in your life, but the Lord has always been with you. Because of these things, He has been able to bless you with great gifts." Because it happened and because I sought God in my trials, He blessed me with Christlike qualities that gave me strength to endure.

I had felt the effects of the Atonement and dedicated myself to God. Next I could begin my emotional and spiritual growth. I may have been twenty-six years old, but I was starting from the beginning—as a child when the abuse began and my emotional growth ended. This time I would fill my gaps the right way. I knew God would lead the way. He had been my protector and teacher thus far, so I had no more reason to doubt I could handle whatever came next.

Emilism: You don't fully understand who you are—a queen, greater than all God's creations.

I took a deep breath of the crisp air coming from the purple-hued mountain peaks. I had returned to the inlet I looked upon eight years before when thoughts of Tom filled my heart. The coastline off the edge of a small cliffside showcased downtown Anchorage at the opposite end. The city skyline met the water and the beach full of sticky sand deposited by glaciers that surround the area.

With the sun shining on the flowing tide and the tall magenta fireweed blowing in the wind, these creations whispered to me that I was part of them. I was God's creation. And like all of God's creations I bore testimony of His love and power. "The Spirit itself beareth witness with our spirit, that we are the children of God" (Romans 8:16).

Whisperings of the Spirit became familiar and God's presence constant as I went about my days. I spent so much of my life desperately wanting God's love that I was motivated to never miss a chance to listen to His voice. I began developing a relationship with the God from whom I had been estranged.

While shopping at the local grocery store, I grabbed a small blue notepad and tossed it in my basket. Ninety-seven cents later it was tucked away in my purse for safekeeping because I never knew when inspiration would come.

When God speaks and you listen, the Atonement is at work. I quickly scribbled the words in my notebook before the streetlight in front of me turned green. While my notebook filled up, I didn't always understand what these whisperings meant, but I took time to ponder each one. They would provide guidance, comfort, and speak peace to my heart.

Curiously, I kept hearing the word *truism* over and over, so that it began to stick in my mind. It was strange how many people were using this word. Over time I realized my insights were also truisms—personal truisms. *Things I find to be true about myself—weaknesses that surface and/or virtues I possess, all of which play out in my life in different ways, shaping my character and ultimately putting me on the road to happiness.* I opened my notebook and on the cover page spelled out the word *Emilism*.

Emilism: You are a servant, a leader, and a protector. You are a healer, you are a vessel, you are a light.

"[L]ove the Lord thy God with all thine heart, and with all thy soul, that thou mayest live" (Deuteronomy 30:6). I already knew the girl who grew up in southern California: captain of her swim team, good student, physically attractive, the pianist, the cook, the perfectionist. That girl knew nothing more about happiness than a baby who cries at every whim dependent upon rescue from some unknown source. I had tried unsuccessfully to put my life back together using those traits, but eternal value cannot be found in temporal things. They are all true, but only a matter of circumstance. They don't define who I am any more than does being a victim of sexual abuse.

As I began to know God, I began to know His daughter Emily, the real Emily, the spirit daughter who chose to come to this earth and face the refining process. My Emilisms were more than a sum of my strengths, weaknesses, and experiences. They revealed my divine nature, my eternal value defined by spiritual gifts and talents inherited from God, which nothing and no one could take from me. "Behold thou hast a gift, and blessed art thou because of thy gift. Remember it is sacred and cometh from above" (Doctrine and Covenants 6:10).

Each whispered revelation peeled back a layer of guilt, sin, or regret and gave me a glimpse into my soul. Underneath those layers I discovered someone I loved. Someone who was contemplative, meek, quiet, smart, mellow, sensitive, empathetic, reserved, strong, happy, peaceful, intuitive, bold, confident, and beautiful. In these moments of perspective, the door to God opened a crack and I was able to reach through and experience the happiness I desired.

Not immediately, but in due time, peace replaced depression, and my need to binge and purge passed. I came to know the Spirit as a trusted friend and companion. The bonds the world placed upon me were replaced with a true self-esteem developed in faith. In time the labels the world gave—victim, bulimic, broken—gave way for the title: daughter of the most high God.

CHAPTER 9

[R]emember that faith is always pointed toward the future.
... [I]t is not right to go back and open some ancient wound
that the Son of God Himself died to heal. ... Faith builds
on the past but never longs to stay there.
Jeffrey R. Holland (5)

Emilism: The path must be cleared.

One year came and went. Life's seasons changed and the fresh white dust on the mountains gave the wind a crisp bite. Not only was the Spirit my constant companion, but so was change. Tom finished his college degree online and settled into a job while I settled into the routine of motherhood. The next logical step was to purchase a home. Tom began the process by looking for the best investment, but I knew I needed to fall in love with a house in order to make this commitment. Home is my favorite place to be. So for me it was not just about making an investment, but what that house would represent: peace, safety, security, and love. I expected to walk in the front door and receive a moment of clarity and confirmation that it was meant to be.

Exploring our options, we picked up every house ad we could get our hands on. We flipped through hundreds of listings and strolled through countless open house showings. We talked about what we wanted and didn't want. Neighborhoods, schools, friends, wards.

We weren't sure where this search would lead. I knew the right home was out there, but I didn't know where I would find it or how long it would take. The home was going to be a physical dwelling for my family, but I was also searching for lasting happiness for myself. I knew it was on the other side of that door where God waited for me to enter, but I couldn't seem to keep it open long enough to get through.

Emilism: You cannot be happy when you are the victim.

Being abused was not my choice. So many precious things were stolen from me in that most secret moment. My agency along with my virtue, self-worth, and trust. The effects were massive, rippling throughout my life, but not every choice was taken from me. My choices could create the home environment my family would live in. I could fill the rooms with sadness or peace, self-loathing or love, isolation or hope, fear or faith.

I found myself standing on the cliffs of life. I shivered as I contemplated the leap of faith it would take to leave the victim standing on the edge. This leap meant so many things: moving forward, letting go, leaving the past behind, putting my faith and trust to the test. Fear kept me paralyzed on the edge. Fear kept me trapped in the past—fear of facing the pain and the work it would take to heal. *What if there was nothing there to catch me?*

The longer I stood on the edge the louder the victim's voice became and the farther the leap felt. She didn't want to let me go. If I did, then who would tell her story? She demanded to be heard, but her voice was one of confusion calling me back to my old ways and causing me to doubt my faith.

I'd read the Book of Mormon several times by now and was familiar with its message. This scripture in Moroni 10:32 became my favorite. In this scripture, I saw hope for a better future. I saw a strength I did not yet possess.

> *Yea, come unto Christ, and be perfected in him, and deny yourselves of all ungodliness; and if ye shall deny yourselves of all ungodliness, and love God with all your might, mind and strength, then is his grace sufficient for you, that by his grace ye may be perfect in Christ; and if by the grace of God ye are perfect in Christ, ye can in nowise deny the power of God.*

Moroni used the word perfect, a word I struggled with in the past. I imagined complete perfection as something to be achieved in the next life, but Moroni's words urged me towards the edge with a message that if I let go, grace would be there to catch me.

When I heard the front door open, I was busy putting dinner on the table. Tom kissed me and asked his usual question, "Did you have a good day?"

It was a habit to reside in my negative feelings. They had been around for so long, like an old dysfunctional friendship. In the back of my mind I constantly searched for something to be upset about. Although my deepest desire was to be happy that feeling was foreign to me and felt strange to express.

I made a conscious decision to smile and say, "Yes. I had a good day." Choosing not to give voice to those negative feelings that lingered in the back of my mind, choosing not to give into the victim.

A price-reduced sticker was posted on a bank-owned property. Tom and I were excited to find a house that we thought would fit within our tight budget.

We wandered through the fixer-upper. Tom saw potential where I saw a money pit. The house had been on the market for five months so we felt confident our offer would be accepted. If we could get a good price, we would have money left over to do the necessary work, but I had no moment with that house. It was not the wrong decision when we put in our offer, but one of blind optimism. We were cramped in our tiny apartment and ready for a bigger home.

Our lives needed a lot of fixing up as well. There was still much to be salvaged and pieced back together with no quick fix. The potential was exciting, but the task seemed overwhelming.

To our surprise within twenty-four hours two other offers were submitted. We had a chance to change our price to be more competitive, but during those hours I developed an infection and a high fever. I was in no shape to make serious decisions. We were outbid and lost the house.

Although the bank-owned property was not meant to be, for the first time our dreams of owning a home were becoming a reality. At the same time our dreams of an eternal marriage were unfolding.

After going through the steps of repentance Tom still found himself struggling with feelings of guilt, not just over turning to pornography, but for many of the decisions in his life he viewed as regrets or failures.

We put the home magazines on the shelf to make time to read scriptures together. Tom's familiar voice read Alma's words:

> *And I also thank my God, yea, my great God, that he hath granted unto us that we might repent of these things, and also that he hath forgiven us of those our many sins and murders which we have committed, and taken away the guilt from our hearts, through the merits of his Son.*
> *Alma 24:10*

He stopped there. This scripture held little weight for me, I was just going through the evening ritual, but he later told me that in the silence he made the last step in his repentance process. He allowed himself to experience the full effects of the Atonement. He saw himself holding tight to a bundle of helium balloons filled with guilt. He knew God had forgiven him, but wasn't sure what it meant to forgive himself. The answer was simple, open his hand and let the guilt float away.

That night he bowed his head and asked for the one thing he'd always been afraid to ask for—humility. In the words of this scripture Tom asked God to remove the guilt from his heart. What he got in return was grace filling him with love and power. The spiritual strength I had always admired was restored and our life together took a turn for the better.

Emilism: Following the Spirit promotes personal growth.

Mother's Day came two weeks before I was due to give birth to our third child, another daughter. In the morning I found a beautiful white orchid in full bloom sitting on the kitchen table. I love plants, especially during the dark Alaskan winters. Inevitably the life of the blooms came to an end. At this point most people discard the foliage, but I had faith in my little plant and was determined to see it bloom again.

I typed "re-bloom orchid" in the search bar of my internet browser and read through the postings. I peeked at the roots before each watering to check the moisture, moved it around to make sure it got enough sunlight, and gave it the right fertilizer. The following spring, I carefully twisted my orchid out of its pot, rinsed off the roots, trimmed back the dead parts, and then tucked them back into a new bed of orchid bark.

The scriptures often compare building faith to a seed. If nourished it will grow day after day, year after year. I couldn't see the progress I was making inside, but I was dedicated to my spiritual growth. When I needed light, I knelt in prayer. When I needed water, I reached for my scriptures. When I needed fertilizer, I attended the temple. When I needed repotting, I partook of the sacrament and sought forgiveness.

This little plant has no roots,
Its potential still to show.
But with sunshine, water, and TLC,
A beautiful plant it will grow.
Much like a testimony, this little plant,
We have much growing to do.
So do those things you know will help,
Build a testimony strong and true.
Search, ponder, and pray we were taught,
In Primary not so long ago.
Nurture your testimony with these three things,
Apply them as you go.
When your roots have grown strong,
After much labor and toil,
Your light will shine brighter,
Firm in gospel soil.
So put this little plant in your window,
And as you nurture it with love,
Let it always remind you,
Stay close to your Father above.

Losing this bank-owned property was for the best. Financially the house would have drained us, and shortly after Tom was laid off from his job at the local newspaper. Our progress was halted for a time. We couldn't have any house until we could financially sustain it, and I couldn't sustain lasting happiness until I learned to consistently make healthy choices.

CHAPTER 10

Marvel not that all mankind, yea, men and women, all nations, kindreds, tongues and people, must be born again; yea, born of God, changed from their carnal and fallen state, to a state of righteousness, being redeemed of God, becoming his sons and daughters; And thus they become new creatures; and unless they do this, they can in nowise inherit the kingdom of God.
Mosiah 27:25-26

Emilism: The laws of God are fulfilled as you walk in righteousness.

Tom took a job as a manager in a commercial print shop thirty minutes away in a small town tucked under the shadow of the Chugach Mountains. Tom fell in love with the area and proceeded to convince me it was the place to be. After much persuading, I agreed to look at homes there, but it was a difficult decision. I would be leaving the familiarity, and therefore security, of my life in Anchorage.

A short sale was listed down the street from the print shop. I was apprehensive about getting involved in a short sale, but a previous buyer rescinded their offer a few hours before we showed up. I took this small window of opportunity as a sign. This house also needed some work, but much less than the one before. Our realtor stayed up late that night to get an offer ready to submit first thing the next morning.

On the drive back into Anchorage I felt the Spirit settle into my heart and mind. The radio was off, the kids quiet in the backseat, and we drove home in silence as I enjoyed feelings of peace. The only clear message was that God loved my family. I knew I was on the right track, but I still wasn't sure if that was the moment of surety I sought. This prompting was more about opening up to change.

Our offer was accepted. We mentally moved in and made all sorts of plans. In my mind, walls were knocked down and the kitchen expanded, the overgrown yard cleared. I imagined heavy machinery digging out a path to hang a door that would connect the garage to the house. Pictures hung, furniture arranged, and the forty-year-old house was transformed into a new and more purposeful home. Like this short sale house, I spiritually needed clearing, remodeling, and expanding. I needed a new heart, new eyes, and a new attitude.

Emilism: The cure for spiritual dyslexia is developing your spiritual eyes.

I sat with my back against the edge of my bed and flipped my scriptures open to the page marked from the previous day.

The light of the body is the eye; if, therefore, thine eye be single, thy whole body shall be full of light. But if thine eye be evil, thy whole body shall be full of darkness. If, therefore, the light that is in thee be darkness, how great is that darkness!
3 Nephi 13:22-23

I scanned my room with the brown eyes I was born with, my physical eyes. They focused on the unmade bed, the basket of dirty clothes, and unorganized closet. I was reminded of my day ahead and chores that needed to be done.

Over my lifetime I've watched the temporal world rush by. People always busy with one task or another, making demands, being selfish, and acting out of fear. Tom loves my brown eyes, but they have created doubt and confusion as they led me through a world of hypocrisy. I learned to judge others and acted in ways to shield myself from the injustice. My eyes have one defect, they cannot see what is beyond their immediate understanding.

However, inside this physical vessel are another set of brown eyes that belong to the spirit daughter. These eyes looked at the daily tasks as opportunities for growth, service, and the comfort of possibilities. Instead of confusion, they use their understanding of eternity to build faith. These spiritual eyes have guided me through life's challenges in ways that my physical eyes could not, helping me understand what cannot be seen. They recognize that justice is a flowing and eternal source powered by the love of God and His laws.

I grabbed my notebook titled Emilism and turned to a fresh page. At the top I wrote, "Spiritual Eyes". Then the most subtle whisper of the Spirit urged my pen across the paper.

—Seeing others as Christ does, developing charity, seeing their qualities and worth.

—Seeing miracles.

—Having complete faith.

—Gratitude, seeing God's gifts and blessings.

—Learning the lesson in adversity.

—Seeing everything, every circumstance, every hour and minute as an opportunity from God.

—Drawing strength from the Savior and applying the Atonement.

—Believing all is possible with God.

—Giving God credit.

—Seeing that you are a beautiful and tender daughter of God.

I ripped the sheet out of my notebook and taped it to the inside of my scriptures. I promised myself to read it every day for one year. This habit opened my heart to change and began to develop my spiritual eyes. By relying on them I began to see the world in a whole new way. Not because the world was changing, but because I was.

These changes transformed me and my relationships with the people close to me. I saw Tom in a whole new light. And not only him, but my parents as well. I began to see their strengths and the love they had to offer me. The things that hurt me in the past began to fall to the wayside. In fact, many things began to fall to the wayside. By using my freedom to choose the direction my life was going, my agency was being restored.

Emilism: Moments of peace make life worth living.

While it was true I put my trust in God, gave Tom my love, and made a promise to my son, I continued to view men generally in a poor light. That changed one summer evening when the midnight sun was up and the kids were down for the night. I placed a disc into the DVD player, a random selection from Netflix.

The movie was about a twelve-year-old boy who, with the help of a prison guard, escaped from a labor camp after the second world war. On his journey across enemy territory, he learned many life lessons as he was influenced by the people with whom he came in contact.

As I watched the movie, I was moved by the portrayal of this boy. Faced with many obstacles he showed a moral courage few possess. By the end, when he was reunited with his mother, I was sobbing, overcome with compassion. I was able to see a young boy the way Heavenly Father may, as someone innocent and pure, ready to grow into a man, still needing to be loved. This was something I had never been able to do, becoming yet another special tender mercy from my Father in Heaven.

In a single moment, I shed the perspective my physical eyes

had created over years of experiences. My spiritual eyes made it possible for me to completely change the way I saw men. This experience was solidified when I picked up the sleeve to replace the DVD and read my brother's name in the title. A little piece of my heart softened towards him. I wondered at what point he turned from the innocent boy he once was to the person who was able to cross the line into my bed.

Emilism: You cannot pray and ask God to make your life easy.

After waiting five months for the short sale house, I got a phone call from our realtor letting me know that the sellers pulled out of our contract. We were left empty-handed, but I still believed that somewhere out there was a place for my family.

The day after we lost the short sale Tom was offered a job in the valley roughly forty-five miles from Anchorage. The local newspaper wanted him as their ad director, a huge promotion. It would provide the financial means to purchase not a bank-owned or short sale property, but a beautiful new home. The only problem was I would again be sacrificing the security of my life in Anchorage for a whole new experience. I wrestled very much with the idea of moving so far away. Tom promised he wouldn't sign a contract until I was sure I wanted to move. It seemed to be our best option, so I went on the search.

As the road turned away from the mountains, the valley was stunning on a clear day. I was full of hope with the ads I had printed tossed on the passenger's seat. One home in particular I was excited to see. I didn't have an appointment, but when I drove by the house the owners were in the yard and invited me in.

Everything about it felt wrong. The ceilings were uncomfortably high like an old haunted house. The wood floors were scratched and old, the carpet stained, the kitchen worn. It didn't look anything like the picturesque ad, and it didn't help that the neighborhood swarmed with mosquitoes.

This was my fifth trip to the valley and every time was a painful process. I spent a ton of gas money driving back and forth, looking at houses, looking at lots, talking to builders, trying to imagine myself living there, thinking about the changes it would bring. Every time I drove the forty-five miles out, I was filled with so much hope. Every time I drove the forty-five miles back, I cried the whole way home.

I let go of my hope and discouragement took over. Spiritually I crashed. I turned to God and demanded to know "Where Can I Turn for Peace?" (Hymn #129).

Dear Heavenly Father,

My mind has been very cluttered lately. When I pray the words won't come to my mind, and it just feels like a mess in my head. I have many unanswered questions that are running around in my mind.

I am trying to be what you want me to be. I am trying to learn and listen. Is there something that I am missing? I constantly come back for more. I go through these spiritual ups and downs. I suppose that is normal. When I am up it is hard for me to imagine that it will ever end. I feel so confident. I wonder how my faith could ever be shaken, but without fail, and so easily it seems, something will come into my life that tips the balance in the other direction. When I get in the slump my mind becomes very clouded and confused. It is probably normal because it keeps me turning towards you, but I hate the distance it creates between us. You are the source of all my strength and hope, so I feel very weak when I do this.

There have been a lot of obstacles to overcome. After all the heartache I have been through, I just want my life to mean something. I want to mean something to you. Of course the thought occasionally runs through my head that I might have this all wrong. Please guide me. Please show me. Please care for me. Please cherish me. Please open my eyes. Help me feel the Spirit and know that you are there. Please help me in my weakness.

It seems that the questions and answers are right there just out of reach and you are waiting to give them to me, I am just not quite sure how to get them. Are you waiting for me to understand?

Love,

Emily

I wanted God to just fix everything. I had complete faith that He could. There were certainly times when He had swooped in and saved me, but a part of me believed God's deliverance was the only thing that could help me up when I fell. But without any effort on my part, my leap of faith would have fallen short of the courage required to fill the remaining gaps. "Were you to receive inspired guidance just for the asking, you would become weak and ever more dependent. ... [E]ssential personal growth will come as you struggle to learn how to be led by the Spirit" (Richard G. Scott [6]). He stayed His hand until I worked up the strength to pick myself off the ground. This was the only way for God to teach me how to open the door myself.

After a good cry, I picked up the listings and began my house search all over again. This time with a little more knowledge, more experience, and a clearer path.

Throughout this time, Tom and I remained in the small south Anchorage apartment, but other changes inevitably came. Each passing year brought its own set of trials. My daughter went to the emergency room with a broken leg, Tom's father was diagnosed with Alzheimer's disease, family members passed away, disappointments came, appliances broke, money was tight, feelings were hurt, battles were fought. I faced many storms, large and small. With each new trial, I got better at trusting God, better at having faith and letting go, better at recognizing God's hand in my life and His direction. As I applied these changes, I looked back and realized that with each passing year I became more steadfast. I was building a true foundation.

Although I still did not have a key to my own home, the Spirit was the key to opening the doors to my heart—the key to change.

CHAPTER 11

For all the law is fulfilled in one word, even in this; ...
LOVE.
Galatians 5:14 (emphasis added)

Emilism: You have so much love to give, though you have
not discovered it yet. You must learn to love!

I was at a point where I was doing really well, secure in my
faith and testimony, and I truly enjoyed my service at church. I
even went long periods of time without thinking about my
"troubled" past. This was great progress considering I spent
years letting it consume me. Now that I understood God's love
for me, I began to see patterns of how His love shaped me and
recognized this as the Atonement at work.

Things seemed to be coming together, but this progress
was not enough. Love and trust are built together, so even
though I was developing this relationship with God, I still did
not trust the world around me. I shut people out as a way to
protect my tender heart.

Dear Heavenly Father,

I sometimes wonder just how messed up I am. I desperately long to be loved. Am I unable to feel it at this point in my life? Have I been so damaged that I am incapable of feeling loved even when someone does try to love me? How deep do the wounds of abuse and neglect run? I feel loved by you when I feel the Spirit, but sometimes it is hard for me to feel it and sometimes when I do, I don't trust it. A lot of times I just feel like a big nobody.

Love,

Emily

I spent so much time feeling isolated and unloved that I did not know how to connect with and love other people. It was easier for me not to participate in social groups because I felt like they couldn't possibly understand me. My testimony had grown into something strong and true, but I kept myself closed off from those who were not in my inner circle. This behavior also kept me from the vital support and love I needed.

I pulled my Emilism journal off the shelf and tucked it under my scriptures. I turned the pages through the epistles of Paul. His testimony resembled that of Alma's. Through God's mercy he turned a life of sin into a testimony of redemption.

Paul really knew something about love. As I read, I marked each passage of love and made a list.

—God's love is perfect and unchanging for all His children.

—True love is not won, it is given. Finding love is not a contest.

—God's love provided the Atonement. Our love for Him applies the Atonement to us and unites us with God.

—Love is healing.

—The love of God is felt through the Holy Ghost.

—The love of Christ/God will make you conqueror of all tribulation, distress, persecution, famine, nakedness, peril or sword.

—Love is the foundation.

—If you have a testimony of and understand God's love for you, you will find strength to endure.

—There is nothing you can do, good or bad, that will change God's love. His love is perfect and unchangeable. Remember this and you will not be so concerned with every little step you take, only that you continue walking in the light.

—Charity/love is the greatest of all virtues.

—Do not serve others out of necessity, but out of love.

—Don't assume that the people in your life know that you love them, tell them.

—Charity is the pure love of Christ.

—When the opportunity comes, we will recognize Christ through and by the love/charity in our hearts.

—Every commandment hangs on the principle of love.

—God's love is the fountain of youth, it restores.

—Love is the measure of faith.

—Love is safety.

—Accepting what people have to give is love.

—Love is the glue that holds the gospel together.

—Finding God's love is the process of being made whole.

—Love is how the Atonement takes effect in our lives.

—God's love gives our lives purpose.

—GOD'S LOVE WILL MAKE YOU WHOLE!

As my list came together, I reflected on my life. Each time I was blessed with God's love, whether in small or significant ways, a little piece of my heart was healed. It could have just been a comforting feeling, a blessing, a prompting from the Spirit, a scripture I read, or one of the more significant moments when God's grace pulled me out of the darkness. With each piece my heart was restored, not to its original form, but to a new form God had created. "A new heart also will I give you, and a new spirit will I put within you" (Ezekiel 36:26). I did not become the person I always yearned for, a flawed version of perfection, but the person God wanted me to be, the daughter He had thoughtfully gifted with eternal qualities.

In each healing moment, I learned something new and took another step towards God and towards becoming united with Him.

Emilism: When we feel love it heals us; when we give love, we become Christlike.

"All ... can be filled with love, knowing that their small acts of charity have a healing power for others and for themselves" (Silvia H. Allred [7]). Throughout my life particular people have crossed my path. The people I feel most connected to are not necessarily the people I have the most in common with, but the people who have offered me Christlike love, which is called charity (see Moroni 7:47). Charity bonds people together. We may have only exchanged a few words that stayed with me or they may have always been present, but either way their influence has helped me navigate the trials of my life.

During the Christmas season on one particularly discouraging day I was in the store and knew I had a tear in the corner of my eye. I was feeling overwhelmed by the temporary stresses of that week. A very kind man helped me with my groceries and then warmly wished me a merry Christmas. Afraid I might start crying in front of him, I could hardly muster up a thank you. I hope God blessed him with something special that day. He will never know how big his small act of service was to me.

During my third pregnancy, I suffered from severe morning sickness. I lay in silence most of the time, trying to hold back the nausea by keeping my mouth shut tight. I spent months confined to the couch. My visiting teachers brought meals for my family and sat next to me with empathy in their eyes. It made my confinement seem less lonely. Every time I told them how much I appreciated their help during that time they shrugged it off. They thought they didn't do much, but just sitting with me relieved some of my discomfort.

One of my cousins has always had a presence in my life. I've watched her over the years, quietly going about serving others without a thought of recognition. Her Christlike example has motivated me to be a better person.

Years ago, I found myself singly trying to organize my first big activity for the women in my ward. As I collapsed on the couch, overwhelmed with the task, my phone rang. A woman I barely knew asked me for a list of things I needed and told me she would pick me up Saturday morning. No one asked her to help, but she stayed the whole day to set up, organize, and even clean up. She saved me that day.

God's love is the key ingredient in the Atonement, but His love is not limited to my inner circle. I was never going to feel loved until I faced my own issues preventing me from connecting with people. These moments, when someone else brought God's love to me, were also healing moments. I realized there was still so much good in the world. If I could put my trust in Him then I could also put my trust in the people who emulated His love. If I truly gained a testimony of God's love for me, then I needed to find a way to express the love I felt to my neighbor as well. "[U]nless we lose ourselves in service to others, there is little purpose to our own lives" (Thomas S. Monson [8]).

I looked for opportunities to perform small acts of charity. My uncle went into the hospital for a simple surgery and came out with a devastating diagnosis. He had terminal cancer and was given a few short months to live. This news was especially hard on my grandfather.

Grandpa's birthday was coming up, which inspired me to make a very special gift. I pulled back the lid on my electronic piano, plugged in a flash drive, and set a thick book of waltzes against the stand. I spent hours recording his favorite songs, making each note perfect. This was, after all, what I had trained myself to do. But this time the gift I gave was not to prove that I was worth loving, but to be a vessel for God's love.

Using my computer, I loaded the songs onto a CD. When I handed my grandpa my handmade gift, he sobbed like he had sobbed so many times for his dying son. He held me in a tight embrace. "This is the best gift anyone has ever given me."

Over the next three months as my uncle's death approached, my grandpa was stricken with grief. He told me every time he felt down, he put in the CD I recorded for him and my music would help him through the unbearable moments.

I was able to use my talent to bring peace to my grandpa during his time of suffering and grief. It was a gift of love that blessed me and him. For me a gap was filled and as a result, grandpa received a tender mercy from the Lord.

I finally understood the true meaning of love. The patterns woven by accepting and giving love worked together to produce one amazing and intricate design. "Love is a potent healer" (Richard G. Scott [9]). Whether from a personal connection with God or from a bond of charity with someone else, anything that brought God's love to my heart was a healing moment.

Emilism: A heart that knows love sees God in everything.

Continuing the house hunt, Tom and I made the drive to the valley together one Saturday afternoon. We turned onto Cottonwood Drive because we were told the best schools were in this area. One of our church buildings was tucked inside an inviting neighborhood at the bottom of the mountains known as Hatcher Pass. It was breathtaking.

As we pulled in, I thought, *this is it!* I had *a moment.* It wasn't clear or sure like I had expected *my moment* to be, but I finally let go of my fears and prepared to take the leap of faith. I could imagine myself settled there with the kids playing in the woods and the creek that ran through the back of the available lot. A house built there would give a view of the treetops and be open to all sorts of wildlife. I opened my heart and fell in love with this new home that hadn't even been built yet. My mind was put to rest. The plans were worked up with a builder for a home. It would be a beautiful, brand new home, nothing to fix up, but it would be a new start for our family.

What finally opened my heart to others was accepting a call to lead the women in my ward—a counselor in the Relief Society organization. The members of my ward raised their hands in confidence as my name was called to be given a sustaining recognition, but I stood there unsure if I had enough love to give the women who were in need. I knew my heart was closed and I struggled with feelings of bitterness, thinking how no one was ever there for me during my trials.

This was a huge growing time for me. I learned so much about what happens outside my own perspective. It strengthened my testimony in so many ways, yet at the same time kind of burst the bubble in which I kept myself. The biggest thing I learned was that no matter what trials pass through a person's life, pain is universal. I realized people do not have to have walked my path to feel what I have felt. Life is a challenge for everyone. Everyone feels pain regardless of their unique experiences.

A few weeks after receiving this call to serve I was exercising and taking advantage of the time to clear my mind. I began pondering the paths that brought me to this point and how my new calling would affect my future growth. Thoughts of experiences and paths that built my testimony came pouring into my mind. I grabbed a pen and paper, held it against the stand of the elliptical, and wrote down everything that came to me.

Instead of sorrow that forced my feet against the pavement in darkness years ago, I let this inspiration fuel my movement and fill me with light. I took advantage of the power accessible to me from God. A distinct difference from my past feeble attempts to gain control over my body. This marked a change in the way I sought both power and control.

Fast and testimony meeting was coming up and I knew I needed to stand and share my thoughts, but I was terrified. What I had written would be bearing my heart and soul to my ward. If rejection was the outcome, it could be a devastating blow. But if it went well it could be one of the best things I had ever done.

The morning of our Sunday services my nerves woke me before my alarm. I knew if I didn't get up to the stand I would regret it. Before church I knelt and asked God to provide me with the courage I needed to overcome my fear.

After the meeting was turned over to the congregation, I felt compelled to get up and walk the distance to the front of the chapel. Some unseen influence must have moved my feet one step at a time because against all reason I made it. I began talking about how I gained a testimony. Without sharing details, I described the darkness that was my life, reading the Book of Mormon, seeking God's love, and the experience I had walking into the light.

It was incredible. I knew exactly what to say. The words came out with power and conviction. Once again, another wall in my life fell. This time what was in front of me was a sea of imperfect people, just like me. People yearning for a connection and acceptance just as much as I was—people with open arms and open hearts.

It didn't matter what anyone else had done or not done for me. It was impossible for me to recognize love until I was willing to open my heart. The response from my ward was amazing. People hugged me, cried, and expressed how touched they were. I found a connection. Now I could love God and my neighbor. I gained what I needed and was ready to serve the women in my ward.

* * *

Another ad director job opened in Anchorage. A past colleague of Tom's was hiring for the position and was adamant Tom was the perfect fit for the job. It was not an easy decision as now, from a different point of view, we could see the pros and cons of both sides. It was hard to think about giving up my life in Anchorage, but it was also hard to think about giving up the beautiful spot in the valley, the good schools, the new home, and welcoming neighborhood.

It was down to the wire. The offers were expiring and a contract needed to be signed, either the job in the valley or the job in Anchorage. There were no secure feelings either way, but Tom decided there was less risk staying in Anchorage, so the house hunt was still on.

I had thought the new house in the valley was the end of my search. I thought I put my trust in God, that I was taking the leap of faith. When I opened my heart and learned to love, I thought my healing was complete or that it was good enough. I didn't know there were more steps just around the corner.

The next house we seriously considered was down the street from where we were already living. There was no moment, but it was cheap and easy and we could upgrade in a few years. We made an offer. The next day the owners decided they didn't want to sell after all and they pulled the house off the market. Alas, we remained in our cramped quarters.

At this point I threw my hands up and knew this was completely out of my control. I thought I had left it in God's hands before, but this time I knew for sure God must have a plan I knew nothing about. I let it all go, completely, and thought, *I have done all I can do. What will be will be.* I told Tom I was taking a six-month break from looking, talking, or even thinking about house hunting. "As sovereigns, choosing to yield to the Highest Sovereign is our highest act of choice. It is the only surrender which is also a victory!" (Neil A. Maxwell [10]).

CHAPTER 12

*The essence of the miracle of forgiveness is that it brings
peace to the previously anxious, restless, frustrated, perhaps
tormented soul. In a world of turmoil and contention this is
indeed a priceless gift.*
Spencer W. Kimball (11)

Emilism: Love is the expression that draws God's sons
and daughters to the Atonement.

New boundaries in our Anchorage stake were drawn. This
change moved my family into a new ward and released me
from my leadership position. There were a few weeks in
between when I was not serving in any calling. I was happy and
peaceful, excited about all the things I learned. During those
few weeks, I prayed and asked God for an opportunity to serve
that would help me grow in the ways He needed me to. I never
thought to do this before, pray for a specific calling; I always
just took the ones were offered to me. A few weeks later I was
asked to serve as a leader for the twelve and thirteen-year-old
girls in my ward.

This calling triggered the victim's voice. A great deal of pain swelled up and I couldn't get rid of the thought, *When I was their age, I had my brother in my bed.* They were all such sweet girls, but jealousy stirred in my heart and sadness for what I had lost.

I sat in the bishop's office with the other women in our youth group waiting to be given a blessing in preparation for my new calling. Conflicting thoughts turned over in my mind. As I weighed the good and the bad, I found old pains still existed. I gained a sense of peace knowing this calling was an answer to my prayer. Suddenly I knew exactly what the bishop would say when he placed his hands on my head. "God knows your heart. He knows your struggles. He will give you the answers you are searching for." I cried, but tried to conceal my true feelings.

Afterward I sat and talked to the Young Women's president, whom I was just getting to know. I gave her a little information about how I was feeling and tried to explain my tears. She said to me, "You must have an amazing testimony to share about forgiveness." I didn't say anything because the conversation was filled with other thoughts, but in that moment, I knew I did not have that amazing testimony of forgiveness.

After this new call created such a wrestle within my heart, I was prompted, in the most subtle way, to begin writing my story. I had hundreds of journal entries by now that detailed my life. I didn't know why I felt the need to write a separate story.

I had a quiet hour while my son practiced in his dojo. I opened a new note on my phone and began typing. Then it grew line upon line, precept upon precept, here a little and there a little (see Isaiah 28:10).

The more I wrote, the stronger this prompting became. Soon it was all I could think of. I lay in bed night after night writing and pondering, searching my past, drawing from my heart, and tracing my steps. I went back, all the way back to the moment my life took the treacherous path that brought me to where I am today.

Twenty-seven pages later, I had my first draft. During this time a little green spike had emerged from the side of my orchid. This spike was the first sign of change, the first hint of new life due to my efforts in caring for this plant.

After Tom read it, I told my mom what I had done and nervously sent it off to my parents, not knowing how it would affect them. At this time, we still had not had many of the hard conversations. While it could be a difficult story to read, I thought my testimony of the Atonement reached beyond the hurt.

My mom read it quickly, anxious to hear what I had to say. She was very supportive. Her love and acceptance made me feel validated. It prompted thoughtful conversation in which we were both able to find healing. She finally acknowledged what I always felt, the loneliness of being left behind in California. Being validated brought me a sense of release. My mom shared how she suffered during this time as well, providing me with a different perspective.

My dad stayed up late that same night reading. My mom told me later that she paced up and down the hallway, poking her head in from time to time to see if he was finished. After much anticipation, my mom went into their room. She asked him what he thought. He was speechless and silent for what my mom said felt like way too long. When he finally found some words, he said, "I think she is amazing." It was the first time he heard in my own words what I went through all those years ago.

After all these years, my dad finally giving his approval was what set my feelings of forgiveness into motion. His words of love and encouragement made me feel amazing and gave me the strength I needed to take the one last step.

Emilism: Healing opens the path to forgiveness.

After all my healing and growing there was still something missing. This word has been a huge source of frustration for me: forgiveness. I wasn't sure what to think about forgiveness and struggled with the idea of whether or not I had forgiven my brother. I had many blessings to count and thought I could put the hard feelings on the back shelf. Maybe my choice to be happy and move forward was forgiveness? I wasn't sure. I knew I still wanted my family to take *my* side. I made a lot of progress in my healing, but I still found the need to revisit this from time to time.

I felt like I was force-fed forgiveness at church. Every priesthood leader I turned to gave me the same spoonful. There was and is a strong push to forgive quickly because it is considered Christlike, but I needed to be heard and I needed help first.

I sat at the opposite end of the kitchen counter when my friend asked me if I was grateful for my trials. Personally, I love bold questions that make me think. Being grateful for the growth experienced through trials is an idea I heard at church from time to time. I spent my entire life wondering who I would be if *that* had not happened? After hearing my dad's words, I began to wonder *who* would I be if that had not happened?

Also, for the first time in my life I had a desire to pray for my brother. After all these years of waiting for this moment I didn't want to casually mention him in a prayer in my messy bedroom. I went to the temple and sat on a crisp white couch. A glass chandelier hung from the high ceiling casting a brilliant glow over the room. Although the peacefulness of the temple already created a sense of reverence, I closed my eyes and bowed my head. I asked God to watch over my brother and his family, to take care of him, and help him find his way. I asked God to release me from my burden.

In this moment of forgiveness, I did have a tangible interaction with God—a release. Not a whisper of love or comfort, but it seemed as if the actual chemistry of my body changed, amended in some way. I gained that amazing testimony I had lacked and it was not like anything I had ever experienced before. A testimony of eternal truths can be gained by the Spirit bearing witness, through scripture, another person bearing testimony, a hymn, etc. But gaining a testimony of forgiveness is a deeply personal, private, and incredible interaction with God. It was something only He could do for me. I realized how utterly dependent I was upon His grace, the right kind of dependency that brought unity.

Emilism: Forgiveness is a release; forgiveness is a discovery. It is love and charity, removal of guilt, peace, *happiness, a physical response, a lightness in your heart—a priceless gift.*

It took a few days for these feelings of forgiveness to sink in. I found myself often having a prayer in my heart for my brother and hoping God would forgive him. Even now my brother doesn't know what he has done to me and that makes me sad. He also doesn't know who I have become. The first time the thought came to me, *Please forgive him because he does not know what he has done*, was the moment I understood for myself the scripture in Luke 23:34: "Then said Jesus, Father, forgive them; for they know not what they do."

I truly believe God will and that all will be well.

The scriptures make many references to the feelings of forgiveness: burdens may be light, guilt is swept away, take his yoke upon you, deliver you out of bondage, take away the guilt from your heart (see Alma 33:23, Enos 1:6, Matthew 11:29, Mosiah 29:20, Alma 24:10). I'd read these same scriptures over and over until, when I was prepared to see, my spiritual eyes revealed a mystery to me that had previously been hidden.

I finally found the missing "peace". I finally found my way. This moment pushed the door open and out, never to be shut again. God's will for me came in and completely flooded my life and brought with it my one true wish, more happiness than I could ever imagine. I knew, more than I had ever known, that I was a daughter of God. Everything in my life made sense and became crystal clear.

✳ ✳ ✳

The Christmas tree was up now for the busy season. This testimony came in such a powerful way that I could barely express myself to Tom as we sat under the white glow of the tree's lights. I grabbed my Emilism journal, flipped to the right page, and moved it into his hands. He read my newest revelation: *You are a defender of virtue, a tool in God's hands and in His plan.* He looked up at me and said with complete faith, "Let me introduce you to Emily. The girl I have always known."

The next week I had an opportunity to visit with my grandpa. I sat by him and he took my hand; my hand that I inherited from him and is his mirror image. I told my grandpa I did not want him to leave this world without knowing how much he meant to me, how much I loved him, and that he would always have a special place in my heart. "Something has happened. I have finally forgiven my brother." His eyes teared and he squeezed my hand. Then he said, "I'm so glad Emmy. I'm so glad."

I testify this is a priceless gift. One I am just beginning to enjoy.

Emilism: You are in the right place.

Only three weeks into my house hunting break Tom hesitantly approached me with some photos of a home. I agreed to look *only*. It was raining the day I pulled up, but I love the rain so this was a good sign. I walked in the front door and to my surprise, I got *my moment*. The one I had been searching for the whole time. The one that made all the other moments fade away. Tom went upstairs to talk to the seller while I wandered through the rooms by myself. There was a sense I didn't even need to walk through this house because I already felt at home.

God provided more than I could have ever wanted or needed. But before I could feel at home on this earth, I had to follow His path and learn His lessons. My search sent me digging for answers, knocking on doors, to the edge of my limits, and all the way out to the valleys.

Everything went smoothly with the sale, and amazingly, I got everything I ever wanted. A beautiful home in the same neighborhood with the same schools, same friends, same life. Little did I know the perfect home was within one mile of the south Anchorage apartment we had lived in during our long hunt. So close yet so out of reach until the day I surrendered my will.

CHAPTER 13

The Savior's Atonement ... makes it possible for us to be sanctified. We can then live in unity, as we must to have peace in this life and to dwell with the Father and His Son in eternity.
Henry B. Eyring (12)

Emilism: Acknowledge the hand of God.

Closing day came and time to move in. The kitchen and bedrooms were full of boxes to be organized. I thoughtfully found a place for each of my belongings. My piano was centered next to the staircase where its music would flow throughout the house. I hung a picture of Christ on the mantel above my new brick fireplace. I tucked my plants in spaces I thought they would thrive. These are not just belongings, but symbols of who I am, each one telling a story of its influence in my life.

During the dark winter days, the plants I care for in my home are a reminder of life. They always struggle a little, but as soon as the sun comes back, they perk right up. When I look at the picture of Christ on my mantle, I remember that He is my friend and Savior. The sun is aglow behind His profile and the water swirls around his feet. He encourages me to have faith.

These reminders and symbols are priceless belongings because even though I have tasted of God's love, when challenges come and my faith continues to be put to the test, it's easy to forget what He has done for me. Even through the ebbs and flows of writing this story, the journal of my life, I have been guilty of forgetting what God has done for me in my desire to move forward more quickly than I am ready. Another part of the process of letting go and trusting God so that His will may be done in me.

With my orchid at full bloom, I set it next to the window that was its backdrop and began to ponder how this little orchid was so very much like myself. It took years to store up the faith I needed to prepare for this healing process. That faith made it possible for me to finally break free from beneath the darkness. Since moving back to Alaska, I have grown and built upon my experiences and taken so much thoughtful care of my testimony. I have drawn strength from my Savior, growing in unison as His Atonement provided my foundation.

Some think of orchids as elusive or hard to grow because of their exotic and delicate flowers. They do have to store up a lot of energy to send up a spike that will bloom, but they are actually a very hardy and versatile plant. With more than 25,000 species they grow all over the world and in many types of climates, from treetops to swamps.

Many different cultures admire the orchid and have given symbolism to this plant—everything from love, beauty, strength, and wealth, to believing it has healing and protective powers. The unusual straight lines and geometric shape of orchids, compared to other flowers, led them to be thought of as a symbol of perfection. The spots on orchids are sometimes used to symbolize the blood of Christ and a new beginning.

The type of orchid I have is a Phalaenopsis. In the wild this species anchors itself to trees or rocks where it can absorb water and nutrients from its counterpart. It grows in unison, drawing strength from a shared foundation.

These belongings, arranged throughout my home, give depth and richness to my life, adding to who I am and will become. They bear testimony of God's presence as I endure to the end. I do not claim to have this all figured out, but at thirty-three years of age my life is finally ready to bloom and I'm so excited to see what happens next.

> *O remember, remember, my sons, ... yea, remember that*
> *there is no other way nor means whereby man can be saved,*
> *only through the atoning blood of Jesus Christ, who shall*
> *come; yea, remember that he cometh to redeem the world.*
> *Helaman 5:9*

Emilism: The war of wills will end when your heart is filled with gratitude.

When I was in elementary school I was teased, as all children are about various things, for my large hands. Embarrassed, I tried to hide my hands from other students. Yes, my hands are large, the skin is rough and worn, my nails are cut short and never manicured. Yet, I have come to recognize my hands as my greatest gift and blessing. Everything good that comes from me comes from my hands. I am not an excellent speaker, but I am good at putting the words of testimony I've gained onto paper. I am not a good singer, but I have mastered the art of playing the piano and I am making significant progress on the organ. I recently picked up drawing and have sketched several temples. My hands are strong, providing service and care for myself and others. I do many laborious tasks for the well-being of my family with no concern for their beauty. I am most profoundly grateful for my hands— the hands others found unworthy.

As my heart turns to gratitude for my blessings and for the ways the Atonement has healed my soul, this virtue fills any remaining gaps in my faith and trust because I believe God will continue to bless me in the future as he has in the past, helping me let go of my will completely and be 100% in His trusting and loving hands.

I'll never forget the day we moved into our home. It was the day before Thanksgiving. There was much to give thanks for that year, but especially for the people who share this home with me. My husband is a symbol of safety and my children a reminder of love. They help guide my faith and inspire me to never give up.

One night we gathered on our soft shag rug under the watchful eye of Christ walking on the water. My son offered these insightful words as he led our family prayer, "We ask that our blessings will make us happy." His own truism—a revelation into the secret of a grateful heart. Those who see blessings see God's hands. "Blessed are the pure in heart: for they shall see God" (Matthew 5:8).

I am grateful for the timing that developed my life's song full of crescendos, decrescendos, fermatas, rests, repeats, and other symbols that create its expression. Each note taken one at a time and given its proper attention. Some answers came immediately, some took ten years, some thirty-three years, and some I'm still waiting for, but now I know God will always prepare a way. He will always be with me, sitting next to me as I play the notes of life; He teaches me the perfect timing of my song.

As I walked to the piano in the front of the chapel for my most recent piano solo, I felt more confident than ever, yet so many feelings still stirred in my heart. Later that evening Tom told me his perspective as I sat down behind the piano. He felt my spiritual strength come through the music I played, but at the same time he had this strange feeling that I might just get up in the middle of the song and walk away. His description was very accurate, it was exactly how I felt.

I played the keys with confidence, just the right amount of control to produce the sound I desired. I didn't care who listened. The keys sang only for me. I know who I am and what I've become. I chose to get up and play that instrument and share my talent.

Many choices in my life limited my agency, but not until I understood what it meant to be 100% united with God did I experience the full measure of the great and eternal gift of agency—until I felt the tug of my weaknesses and still chose to dedicate myself to God, to walk this path, and open my heart. Now I know I will always choose Him no matter what. I have nothing more to prove. I have overcome the test of my agency and the agency of others.

Blessed art thou, Nephi, for those things which thou hast done; ... and hast not sought thine own life, but hast sought my will, and to keep my commandments. And now, because thou hast done this with such unwearyingness, behold, I will bless thee forever; and I will make thee mighty in word and in deed, in faith and in works; yea, even that all things shall be done unto thee according to thy word, for thou shalt not ask that which is contrary to my will.
Helaman 10:4-5

Nephi dedicated himself to God and proved himself worthy. Although he felt sorrow for the people who chose otherwise, he was united with God in such a way that he would never ask anything contrary to God's will. For this he was blessed with strength beyond his own capacity.

Miracles happened after my bishop placed his hands on my head and followed the prompting to promise me my questions would be answered. Through the process of writing this story, I did find the answers to *all* my questions. They had always been there within my own heart if I was simply willing to make an honest search deep in my soul, underneath all the layers. It is there that God's Holy Spirit resides.

The only question remaining is what more can I give to be a more profitable servant. I have no secrets or gaps. Now I can say I am not only 100% united with my Father in Heaven, but 100% happy with my life. I wouldn't change one thing about my past, present, or future because I have, as Alma expressed, experienced joy as exceeding as was my pain, and it is all amazing. It is all beautiful this thing called life, the journey to immortality and exaltation.

Dear Heavenly Father,

Thank you for lifting me out of the shadows, for your grace and mercy, for tenderly watching over me and holding my hand, for your love and guidance, for patience and forgiveness, for your son, my brother, a true brother, the hero of my story.

Please protect me from the influences of the Adversary. Send the Holy Spirit to be with me, to guide and lift me up. Bless me with a grateful heart and with humility. Help me never forget, to live in remembrance, to walk in the path you have provided for me. Forgive me for the weaknesses that hold me back, cause me to doubt or misunderstand. Protect my heart. Set me free to find my calling. Help me see miracles unfold, but no matter how big or small the ask, I know that you know what is best— that ultimately I am subject to your will and not my own. I miss you desperately. Take me home, in your time.

Love,
Emily

CHAPTER 14

*That the trial of your faith, being much more precious than
of gold that perisheth, though it be tried with fire, might be
found unto praise and honour and glory at the appearing of
Jesus Christ: ... Receiving the end of your faith, even the
salvation of your souls.*
1 Peter 1:7,9

Emilism: There is room for improvement, but there is no
room for doubt.

After eight months of growing and blooming the flowers
on my orchid died this week. There are so many things I could
still say, but this story must come to an end. It has consumed
my life during this time and I need to lift up my head and move
forward to the next chapter. I am jumping off and letting go,
hoping God will catch me. I pray my testimony will speak for
itself. "[A]nd when he saw her, he said, Daughter, be of good
comfort; thy faith hath made thee whole. And the woman was
made whole from that hour" (Matthew 9:22).

Six years have passed since touching ground and returning home to Alaska, fifteen years since I told my secret to my parents, and twenty-one since the abuse ended. The organic way in which this book came together, and the blessings of forgiveness and wholeness that it led to, have been no less than a miracle. Even so, there are still many unmarked paths ahead of me, and I have so much to learn. I'm not perfect and sometimes find myself revisiting things I thought I let go of, but as I've learned many times over healing is not a straight path.

Doubts plagued me throughout this process, worries if writing this story was the right thing to do. As the prompting to write grew stronger, so did my fears about how this project would come together and how my words would affect people.

In the beginning, I kept this project close to my heart and only shared it with a few trusted people. Now I feel the same gentle urge as I did in the beginning, to share my testimony with others. These words are my heart and soul and I'm revealing them to the world. I've put so much thought and consideration into them and it scares me to think people may misuse or misunderstand them. Just like house hunting and healing from sexual abuse, each walk of faith has its own ups and downs—a rush of faith and inspiration, followed by moments of doubt and fear.

One morning, during those first weeks of writing, I slid out of bed and onto my knees to pray and ponder my blessings. Upon asking for relief my doubts drifted away. When I stepped out of my room and my husband asked me, "What can I do for you today?" I looked at him and thought about how much our love has grown over the years. I am so grateful to find strength in my husband and in my Savior. They give me the ability to continue on the right path, and in turn, I know I will be able to lift others. "God is my strength and power: and he maketh my way perfect" (2 Samuel 22:33).

My son told me when he feels the Spirit he gets a burst of courage. I think he takes after his mother. It's almost a rush for me to feel the courage that accompanies spiritual promptings, to not know where it will take me, and then to find the treasured blessing at the end of the journey. I feel like the adrenaline junkie that just got back from climbing the highest peak or the marathon runner who dug deep to finish the race. I find it ironic that people jump off the side of a bridge with only a bungee cord strapped to their feet but are not willing to take the same kind of leap of faith with God. The Savior carries me to my highest peak and below all things to my inner strength. "He that ascended up on high, as also he descended below all things, in that he comprehended all things, that he might be in all and through all things, the light of truth" (Doctrine and Covenants 88:6).

We are a funny group of people with our control issues. How foolish of me to not want to let go of the pain and instead let it define me. Until I got my first taste of the Atonement and finally found forgiveness, I never knew who I truly was. Now I can know myself as a whole person because I let go wholly. With each step I have taken in faith He has been there to carefully place my footing.

And whoso receiveth you, there I will be also, for I will go before your face. I will be on your right hand and on your left, and my Spirit shall be in your hearts, and mine angels round about you, to bear you up.
Doctrine and Covenants 84:88

Emilism: You can choose to live life the hard way or with peace and joy.

Healing must take place for all who are involved, which means everyone will have to face their own truth. For this to happen families must be united in the healing process whether abuse has occurred inside or outside the home. This can only happen for those who possess an honest heart.

An honest heart belongs to a person who is willing to examine his or her life in a truthful light, willing to face whatever the consequences may be because he or she hopes for a better future. This person desires change and trusts that overcoming the consequences will bring freedom, peace of mind, and blessings (see Luke 8:15).

Having an honest heart was what allowed me to experience the full effects of the Atonement. In turn I've strengthened my marriage, my love for my three beautiful children, and the power of the Spirit in my home. This refining process has changed every experience I have ever had or will have and the way I interact with and view the world. I've experienced healing in every one of my family relationships, but not all in the ways I expected.

I took a trip with Tom and the kids to visit my parents. We had time to open up and have some honest conversations. It was hard for everyone, but we made a lot of progress. I talked to my parents about my book and shared my testimony of how it came to be, how it was guided by the Spirit. They both appreciated my testimony of the Atonement.

Since then my dad has taken some huge steps on my behalf, for which I will be forever grateful. We stood in the hall when my dad broke down crying and apologized to me. I couldn't help but reach out to hug him, a real hug that melted my heart and filled me with compassion, love, and understanding of the man he is and his role in my life.

I found out my dad actually wrote three letters to my brother, not just the one. I had a chance to read them. They gave me a lot to think about and provided a different perspective of my dad's initial reaction. Everything written was right on point. It seemed my dad had all the right answers, but somehow they were not implemented. That's okay because what I learned from those letters was that my dad does love me and did all that he knew how to do at the time. I've made an effort to contact my dad regularly and nurture that relationship.

My mom was very supportive even when I was feeling weak and vulnerable during my visit. I said things to her I've held back for fifteen years and to my relief she just listened, told me she was sorry, and asked me what she could do now to make it better. The one thing a victim desperately needs is validation, which she has given me. Only God can heal the rest. As the mother of our family she deserves to be appreciated, understood, and above all, loved. She has given her all and no one can ask for anything more.

I had a chance to talk to both my little sisters about the abuse. I'm not sure how big of an impact my abuse had on them. Our age differences made it somewhat removed from their own life experiences. I realized that in the past it would have been better for me to give them some kind of signal I was open to conversation. Nevertheless, whether it was me or them or just life, both my little sisters apologized for not showing me their love and support.

My dad helped me find the courage I needed to tell my brother in person that I had forgiven him. It was terrifying, but liberating at the same time. We will always live on opposite ends of this experience. He appreciated me reaching out. He told me he was sorry for what he did. In fact, he told me he would apologize as many times as I wanted him to. I don't need any more apologies from him. My feelings of forgiveness are a gift from God, a sacred moment, and a place I came to without any strings attached. They have no conditions or expectations, but this goes both ways. While my forgiveness may bring some relief, it has no bearing on my brother's healing process. I don't believe our lives will ever be connected, but I've made my peace.

My older sister was where healing came in an unexpected way. Truth heals hearts no matter how the truth comes to you. After years of trying to make sense of these things, I tried to get to the root of the problem between us by asking her about the night she and my brother convinced me an intruder broke into our home. I also asked about her response when I opened up to her for the first time. She answered with a lengthy letter, claiming the responsibility lay with me because I allowed myself to be manipulated. She felt she had been the victim of the actual lie because she didn't know what took place that first night. She advised me to take responsibility for my own mistakes: for not telling as a young child and for the turn in my relationships after telling, directing me to examine myself as the place where trust was broken. Her tone was that she had done everything possible to help me, but that I was unwilling to recognize and refused to accept her efforts.

Her words had the opposite effect of what she intended. All confusion about our relationship was chased away. I was given a flash of utter clarity. She sees me as broken and there is nothing I can say or do to prove otherwise.

Maybe this sounds strange, but reading her words filled me with joy and spoke freedom to my heart. I had lingered in the past, hoping to find answers from my sister that could heal. Now I could let it go with a clear conscience. I never knew healing could come in such a way.

A dear friend reminded me, "Rejection is protection." This experience led me to understand exactly what these words meant. Through opening my heart I've discovered that those who love me, love me more and those who judge me, judge me more. The blessing in this is I can see clearly where I stand. Being rejected allowed me to let go of unhealthy wants and desires. "And ye shall know the truth, and the truth shall make you free" (John 8:32). I've never felt freer in my entire life than when I forgave my brother and let go of my sister.

I do not advocate holding onto anger, bitterness, or resentment. In fact, the contrary, accepting the weaknesses of others helped me accept my own. In this imperfect world, I've had to put my trust in imperfect people knowing they may let me down, in order to progress. Many Christlike characteristics are developed through relationships with imperfect people: patience, love, service, humility, and more. Whether as a blessing or as opposition, all relationships are sanctioned by God and have a purpose, which is ultimately for each person's refinement. At the same time, having a relationship with God is not dependent upon other people's behavior, nor is healing contingent upon other people changing.

I honor the sacred bonds of family by praying God will restore these relationships in His time. I am so grateful for those people who have been an example to me in continuing to express their love even when I did not recognize it, showing patience, and allowing me to change through this process.

President Dieter F. Uchtdorf said, "It is your reaction to adversity, not the adversity itself that determines how your life's story will develop" (13). In Elder Joseph B. Wirthlin's words, "The question is not whether we will trip and fall but, rather, how will we respond?" (1).

As I healed and let love into my heart, God's truth was revealed to me. Earlier in this story I talked about how I did not have a testimony and never felt God's love when I was growing up. Now I look back upon my journey through the Atonement and can see with my spiritual eyes experiences I was blessed with but did not recognize at the time. What once was an empty childhood is now filled with hope, as is my future.

My house is set the perfect distance just a few miles from the hillside. Every time rain clouds hang on the mountains and the sun shines from the west, a full arcing double rainbow stretches over my backyard. A token sign of God's promise. Evidence that with the perfect combination of trials and hope, a testimony is born.

There are so many years ahead full of possibilities for healing, growth, and change. This story is what has become of my life, but is not the final stamp on me or my family. Looking into the eternities, anything is possible.

PART 2

CHAPTER 15:

PERSONAL MINISTRY

And if men come unto me I will show unto them their weakness. I give unto men weakness that they may be humble; and my grace is sufficient for all men that humble themselves before me; for if they humble themselves before me, and have faith in me, then will I make weak things become strong unto them.
Ether 12:27

Emilism: I'm not quick, but I care.

As I matured through life experiences I grew in my testimony and served in leadership positions at church. My eyes were opened to many walks of life, and other victims' stories started coming my way. I had an honest desire to help and made efforts to reach out to each person, but because victims of sexual abuse have been robbed of their power, they can be very protective of their personal stories.

I find it truly amazing how people approach the trials of their lives so differently. We are all very complex individuals with a unique set of skills and life experiences, and each approach is as unique as the person. In one case a woman buried her experience deep in the past. By doing this she was able to control how people perceived her in the present. When I reached out to her it was unexpected. My sudden intrusion brought up a great deal of emotional trauma. My intention was to offer love and hope and my heart was true. I certainly didn't mean to upset her life and I am sorry for the pain that continues to plague her. For a moment, I felt guilt and sorrow for the pain I caused, but then the following scripture came to my mind.

> *And now, my sons, remember, remember that it is upon the rock of our Redeemer, who is Christ, the Son of God, that ye must build your foundation; that when the devil shall send forth his mighty winds, yea, his shafts in the whirlwind, yea, when all his hail and his mighty storm shall beat upon you, it shall have no power over you to drag you down to the gulf of misery and endless wo, because of the rock upon which ye are built, which is a sure foundation, a foundation whereon if men build they cannot fall.*
> *Helaman 5:12*

At that moment, I appreciated how I was able to build my own foundation, one whereon I could not fall. If my merely mentioning her experience caused trauma, then true healing had not taken place for her.

Dear Heavenly Father,

In a blessing my husband gave me he said my trials have made me who I am today—but who is that? I want to be able to completely shed the things that have clouded my mind since childhood so I can completely understand who I am and have complete faith in myself.

I have always contemplated these things a lot, but lately I realized that I need to understand them clearly so I can move forward. How can I find hope and faith that is constant and will face up to any trial? How can I break through my walls?

You are my all. As always, I am ever dependent.

Your daughter,

Emily

I was in the chapel when I first heard the idea of a personal ministry: *service established by the use of your own personal talents and spiritual gifts, things you can personally do outside of a set calling to build the kingdom of God.* I thought about my life experiences, talents, and spiritual gifts and wondered if I had something unique to offer.

Abuse in any form drives the Spirit away and prevents people from living to their full potential, unless they can find restored hope. I believe my personal ministry is to provide hope to people suffering from abuse, people who have lost hope. To inspire them to find the healing I found through the Atonement of Jesus Christ, my Rock, my Redeemer, my Foundation.

Life is so much more complicated than I can cover in these pages, but this book is my attempt to answer my own question: who am I, and how can I find hope and faith that is constant enough to face up to any trial?

Emilism: You were willing to accept the answer.

Many of these moments are private and personal. Not everyone has a desire to open their heart and share as I have, but the details of my story and my healing moments could belong to anyone. I have opened my heart and exposed my weaknesses to give testimony of God's power. "For the fullness of mine intent is that I may persuade men to come unto the God of Abraham, and the God of Isaac, and the God of Jacob, and be saved" (1 Nephi 6:4).

My experiences have pushed me forward and given me a tender, loving, and willing heart. Here I am bearing it, my heart and soul. I have done it because I have tasted of His love and desire others to know the peace and happiness I have found.

I am also opening my heart to shed light on the reality of the consequences, to give myself a voice, and to give voice to victims out there who feel lost and alone. To validate them, no matter how the details of their experience have played out, for victims who were told it was their fault, for those who have nowhere to turn and have been rejected, for victims who were told, "Well, it could have been worse!" or "It's time to move on." For victims who are still holding onto their secret because they are afraid, for victims who have left the church and turned their backs on God. It's also for people who misunderstand and misjudge these victims, for people who are afraid to have these conversations, for people who picked a side by not picking a side, for those who never lifted a finger to help, and for people that look at me and others as different or unclean.

Over the years there has absolutely been more awareness regarding sexual abuse, but that awareness has come with an ever-increasing occurrence of this horrific act. We live in a society that is destroying virtue and human dignity. In a letter addressed to president of the church, Thomas S. Monson, a district judge declared, "Sexual abuse of children is one of the most depraved, destructive, and demoralizing crimes in civilized society. There is an alarming increase of reported physical, psychological, and sexual abuse of children. Our courts are becoming inundated with this repulsive behavior" (14). I don't think, as a whole, people understand the lasting emotional damage to the victim, their families, and our society.

Statistics can range from study to study, but the National Center for Victims of Crime shows that one in five girls and one in twenty boys is a victim of child sexual abuse (15). Of course, these are based on people who actually come forward and admit to being abused. Many more victims still live in silence.

Emilism: You are not meant to fail.

In every way I am moving forward and putting this behind me, with one exception. As I put the finishing touches on my book, I received a new calling as a Public Affairs Specialist, someone responsible for building relationships and understanding in the community. This calling was timely, as everything is on God's watch. I immediately knew I wanted to get involved in volunteer work with non-profit groups dedicated to preventing violence against women.

Alaska has become known as the rape capital of the US because 37% of Alaskan women report having experienced sexual violence. The Alaska rape rate is two and a half times the national average and child sexual assault is almost six times the national average. It's part of my calling to help church leaders be informed about the issues in our local community. So I have taken on this monster of an issue and become an advocate for victims.

I set up a website: www.restoring-virtue.org. It's meant to provide a place for victims of sexual assault/abuse to find answers, understanding, and experience healing. It's also for spiritual insights and growth taking place beyond the pages of this book. Having a support system is key in the healing process. I hope my voice can be part of the support system whether for a victim, a family member, a friend, a coworker, a church member, or just a bystander.

I am my own person now without the baggage from my past. God has blessed me with the courage I need to do this. It has not been easy getting to this point. I've had to push through walls of fear and climb mountains of doubt. God has put me through spiritual boot camp over the past year. I am learning how hard it is to build the bridge from the idea of taking on a cause to actively doing it.

It's amazing my parents, who once found this topic difficult to even talk about, are now supportive of my book and ask for updates on my work in the community. We have all learned and grown together and come a long way on life's winding path. I want to do anything I can to make my parents proud of me and to honor them. My husband has been absolutely supportive and I can only imagine the blessings God has in store for him for loving me through all of this. I want to be an example to my children and inspire them to find opportunities to serve. I hope they will one day understand why this is so important to me. I believe my work will provide protection for them throughout their lives.

Emilism: You were called to the front lines.

After a long day spent writing, I sat on the edge of my bed with my smartphone in hand and pulled up a video clip of a woman injured by extensive burns. The picture showed her carefully wrapping her scars with bandages before going about her day. Tears dripped down my cheeks as I listened to her testimony of survival and her purpose in life and I thought: *My insides look like her outsides.*

Like this woman, I have come to know that God heals. And like her, my scars continue to cause me pain, but I take special care every day to wrap them in God's love. I do this in a very simple way by practicing my Sunday School answers: daily prayer, scripture study, and weekly church attendance. These things are my protection because, not only is healing not a straight path, it is also not a destination—it is a journey. From time to time, when life gets hard, I have to go back and retrace my steps in order to keep myself on the right path.

One of the differences between me and this woman is people cannot deny her scars. When people look at me or other victims of sexual abuse, they can look right through us. The wounds of sexual abuse are very unique. They are hidden in deep emotional scars.

Because sexual abuse damages the spirit, heart, and mind this is where healing must take place. The cure for abuse is two simple things, love and hope. I believe that while there are some great resources out there, ultimately God restores souls. Healing is a spiritual journey.

When survivors of sexual abuse come together it is like meeting another soldier. You may know nothing else, but the fact you have fought the same battle creates a unique bond.

I have faced so much unexplained and obscure opposition throughout my life. After following the prompting to begin writing and discovering my missing piece, forgiveness, I found a strength of character I never knew I had. I know how to find healing and it is not because I was told by a family member, friend, or counselor. It was through my honest search for a true relationship with my Savior Jesus Christ and Father in Heaven.

Yea, I know that I am nothing; as to my strength I am weak; therefore I will not boast of myself, but I will boast of my God, for in his strength I can do all things. … Now if this is boasting, even so I will boast; for this is my life and my light, my joy and my salvation, and my redemption from everlasting wo. Yea, blessed is the name of my God.
Alma 26:12,36

CHAPTER 16:

RESPONDING TO VICTIMS

[F]or he doeth that which is good among the children of men;
and he doeth nothing save it be plain unto the children of
men; and he inviteth them all to come unto him and partake
of his goodness; and he denieth none that come unto him,
black and white, bond and free, male and female; and he
remembereth the heathen; and all are alike unto God, both
Jew and Gentile.
2 Nephi 26:33

Emilism: You can't give unconditional love until God is enough.

My sweet little brown-eyed girl, my middle child, has always had a strong draw to the homeless population. She is full of questions, so I took her downtown to tour the local homeless shelter. We walked through a darkened room where a dozen women slept on cots.

Whenever the subject comes up of Zion, the Lord's people or the pure in heart, there is thought to be "no poor among them" (Moses 7:18), and the conversation inevitably turns to the homeless. There is often debate about whether or not giving money will help them, or even if they deserve to be there because of bad choices.

Not all poverty is easily detected. The phrase 'no poor among them' encompasses all poverty, sadness, loneliness, broken hearts, and disappointment. Physical poverty is a condition where one has little to no money or lacks in other temporal needs. It often begins in the heart where you cannot see and is intertwined with emotional needs.

Poverty of the heart is also a condition where people are lacking either the ability to feel love or the ability to find happiness because their hearts have been broken. For example, a woman is raped, robbed of her self-worth, rejected, and heartbroken. To cope she buries herself deep in drugs and becomes addicted. To support her habit, she ends up on the street stealing or even selling herself. One day this broken woman wanders over to the street corner with a single bag containing all her earthly belongings and a piece of cardboard in her hand.

Is she a person who deserves to be there or a sister with a broken heart and a broken spirit?

This may be an extreme example, but you can't always know what is in a person's heart or the circumstances which brought about his or her present condition. Anyone could be one tragedy away from homelessness. Yet another reason the Atonement is a vital part of a successful life.

So maybe instead of worrying about the five dollars you should or should not give the person on the street, you could give something that will help them even more, your love.

To truly help a victim of sexual abuse, love and acceptance are the best things to offer. Victims are most confused about love. Some believe the perpetrator loves them, or that others will not love them if they find out.

Victims' ability to heal is directly related to the response of the people around them. When negative, healing is greatly compromised. When offered love and acceptance, it is enhanced. Yet love and acceptance seem to be the hardest things to give when your own heart is filled with anger, fear, pride, hurt, or poverty. "He that loveth not knoweth not God; for God is love" (1 John 4:8).

Love comes from people with honest hearts. It comes from those who understand their divine nature and are willing to open their hearts. It comes from those who are not afraid of their own weaknesses because they are confident in the strength the Atonement provides, and those who are not afraid to be vulnerable or admit they are wrong because they have a desire to be better.

Love is a gift from God and love is putting your trust in Him. It is also a gift we give to others unselfishly expressed through kindness, comfort, and service. It is merciful, letting go of judgments, and long-suffering. Love is *everything* right and good, encompassing every person, principle, virtue, and bond. "Charity never faileth" (1 Corinthians 13:8).

While it is true that only God's love can heal, your love can help draw people to the Atonement and avoid more unnecessary pain. There is no such thing as neutral—there is truth and then there is silence. Silence only increases isolation of the victim, suppresses those healing words, and prolongs the healing process. There is power in truth and honest words. For a victim of abuse being heard equals freedom.

What should be said to a victim of sexual abuse? The answer is simple. "It's not your fault." "I love you." "I believe you." "Thank you for sharing." Loving words, hopeful words, accepting words, honest words—all are healing words. Words that can break down barriers in relationships, show acceptance, build trust, and strengthen love.

Maybe it sounds silly, but love is the cure for so many social maladies. We are always trying to find backdoor ways to fix problems without going to the root because that is where it hurts and that is where it's hard. It's hard to have these conversations, it's hard to not judge others and to offer them the love that makes us vulnerable, but may just be the lifesaver they need.

> [A]s ye are desirous to come into the fold of God, and to be called his people, and are willing to bear one another's burdens, that they may be light; Yea, and are willing to mourn with those that mourn; yea, and comfort those that stand in need of comfort, and to stand as witnesses of God at all times and in all things, and in all places, that ye may be in, even until death, that ye may be redeemed of God, and be numbered with those of the first resurrection, that ye may have eternal life.
> Mosiah 18:8-9

Emilism: This world is desperate for spiritual healing.

Sexual abuse is likely the biggest social and spiritual issue of our day. Gone are the days of dealing with these issues behind closed doors. Sexual abuse thrives on silence.

When abuse is taking place, victims are isolated in a physical and emotional sense. They are manipulated into thinking they are all alone. This is one of the ways perpetrators can gain control over their victims and convince them to remain silent.

As long as we act like this is some huge secret, victims will continue to be afraid to come forward. They are afraid they won't be believed or help won't be available, that they will be judged, or their suffering minimized. We need to talk about it so people feel safe beginning the healing process, so they can experience hope.

With the high and ever-increasing statistics of sexual abuse, chances are you sit next to a victim at church, at school, on the bus, or at work. This does not happen in obscurity. You don't have to look very far to find a life that has been impacted by abuse: a child, a friend, a cousin, a mother, a spouse.

It's unimaginable how many women fall victim to sexual abuse and how destructive it is. Many women struggle their whole lives with the emotional aftermath of abuse with no relief. It saddens me because I know there is a way—a way to replace despair with happiness, anxiety with peace, and fear with confidence. I believe God takes extra special care of His children who have been abused.

If a woman has suffered from sexual abuse or has just been beaten down by the pressures of the world she is often seen as weak, broken, or emotional. It is easy to cast her aside, minimize her suffering, and think she will never amount to anything.

Women who have healed from sexual abuse are a powerful force and influence in God's plan. Healing from sexual abuse builds strength that is unmatched by any other experience because of the effort required to discover one's own self-worth. This sacred and spiritual process can only be done with God and the result is a testimony of unimaginable depth.

A woman may never have to experience sexual abuse firsthand, but our so-called liberated society violates the very nature of women every day by painting them as sexual objects. Women are stripped of their self-worth and bombarded with messages telling them their worth comes from what they do or do not look like.

These influences have created the anti-woman, a sort of equivalent to the natural man (see Mosiah 3:19). She blames the society that created her for all her problems. She lets her sexuality define her and degrades herself by using it to control men. This is the woman who chooses to find power in the things of the world, in things that fade. She believes youth, money, and fame are the ultimate goals. She has left her sacred role in search of equality, but has not found a place among men. Society loves her but real equality has escaped her. Sadly, she no longer defends her rights or the rights of others.

I recently sat in the temple pondering Eve's role as a woman. The thought entered my mind: *Women's rights the right way!* For all the talk about inequality between genders, women really are at the center of everything. They are the center of the family, and the family is the foundation of a healthy society and central to God's plan.

Women are teachers of the future generation, the standard bearers, and the hope and beauty of the world. The proof emerges as everything around her crumbles when a woman is stripped of her virtue, beauty, worth, and strength.

God knows His daughters and He knows what they need. They need to know who He is, of His tender character and deep love for them, of His healing embrace that will provide safety in this troubled world. God needs His daughters to have the strength to hold onto their worth as the world heads down a self-destructive path. Have the tools to fight against the destruction of virtue. Be strong enough to hold their families together. Know how to access the Atonement.

"Awake, my [daughters]; put on the armor of righteousness. Shake off the chains with which ye are bound, and come forth out of obscurity, and arise from the dust" (2 Nephi 1:23).

My mind was turning one night, as it often does, keeping me awake. Thoughts of my children and my future filled the dim room. I remembered the day, all those years ago, I stood with Tom in front of the prophet, Gordon B. Hinckley, wondering what he ever saw in that immature girl. My eyes popped open and it hit me in one powerful epiphany. It was a mother. *A mother in Zion.*

Does God love and value His daughters less than His sons? Such a notion is unthinkable and totally outside the realm of the character of the Almighty. After the Lord created the earth, and everything upon it, He created man. And then, as the crowning act of creation, He created woman. She was the ultimate of all His creations.
Gordon B. Hinckley (16)

A woman is the ultimate of God's creations because she is a mother. The word mother is hard to define, she is so many things, but Adam called his wife's name Eve, "[B]ecause she is the mother of all living" (Moses 4:26). As the first woman, Eve is literally *the mother of all living*. However, all God's daughters are included in this definition by the fact that a mother's first and most important role is to create and nurture life.

Although the greatest thing a woman creates is children, Eve was given the title "mother" before she ever bore a child. Her creative nature was inherent.

This world is full of life. It's breathing, moving, and constantly changing. Mother Nature or Mother Earth is the feminine personification of earth's creative, nurturing, and life-sustaining characteristics. Every daughter of God has been endowed with these same gifts. God's daughters make this world a beautiful place. It's the reason women are so important: a woman nurtures all that is living.

A woman is happiest when she is creating. When she is creating smiles and laughter; when she's creating homes, food, gardens, love, hugs, friendships, stories, testimonies, and peace. She creates the space where people connect with heaven during their journey here on earth.

As a woman and a mother her influence is profound when she is allowed to feel strong and safe in her role as the most valuable of God's creations, the greatest influence for good, the most sacred way of building His kingdom.

A virtuous woman is a woman who is steadfast in her morals and in her faith. She not only cares for her own testimony, but she also cares for and nurtures the testimonies around her. Children will come into her life either by birth, adoption, or simply being a teacher, maybe even as adults because we are all still children in God's eyes. Her divine and unique qualities will shine while preparing for and influencing God's children that come to her.

A woman's eternal worth is discovered through a personal relationship with her Father in Heaven. It is discovered in developing unique talents used to bless and serve. It is discovered in friendships as women uplift each other. It is discovered in seeing her own beauty and maintaining her virtue.

> [T]he moral foundation provided by women has proved uniquely beneficial to the common good. Perhaps, because it is pervasive, this contribution of women is often under appreciated. ... Women bring with them into the world a certain virtue, a divine gift that makes them adept at instilling such qualities as faith, courage, empathy, and refinement in relationships and in cultures.
> D. Todd Christofferson (17)

CHAPTER 17:

TO THE VICTIM

The Lord works from the inside out. The world works from the outside in. The world would take people out of the slums. Christ takes the slums out of people, and then they take themselves out of the slums. The world would mold men by changing their environment. Christ changes men, who then change their environment. The world would shape human behavior, but Christ can change human nature.
Ezra T. Benson (18)

Emilism: The Atonement has no time frame.

There are many standard treatments for abuse including professional counseling and activating a personal support network. However helpful these strategies may be for some people, in my personal journey these treatments proved to be unstable and ineffective. The only thing I remember about the little counseling I had was being advised to write a list of things

I liked about myself. It was not very effective. I didn't believe any of the things I wrote down because inside I felt worthless.

I never had the support or love I needed from family and friends. I know everyone had their own perspective, but no one seemed to know how to help me. I can say at this point in my life that I do not place blame, but at the time I felt completely and utterly alone. Which is why, at the end of the day, my one and only answer was to seek for God's healing while navigating the dark waters of sexual abuse. "Sometimes those who start out the slowest end up going the farthest" (Joseph B. Worthlin [1]).

In sharing my testimony, I wish to help others be prepared and provide a way to overcome the effects of sexual abuse. The truths I've gained took years of soul searching for me to find. If I had known fifteen years ago what I know now, I could have bypassed much suffering.

I've known too many people who are also lost and broken, who do not have an identity and are searching, unsuccessfully, for a way out. Divide and conquer is the Adversary's goal. He would have them believe they do not belong. They were abused so they don't belong, they are addicts so they don't belong, they are unclean, they have no place and will never be accepted. This is where many victims become lost. To them I say: do not think you are too far gone. It's never too late to begin the healing process. "[A]ll is as one day with God, and time only is measured unto men" (Alma 40:8).

Those who have experienced the emptiness of suffering value the gift of salvation more when it is discovered. When they are finally loved, respected, receive light, and find happiness. When you know what it's like to do without, you appreciate what comes because you have to be stronger and work harder. The spiritual strength developed in the process can carry you faster and farther as it refines your soul. The strength of a soul is amazing! Do not underestimate those who you think are weak or behind, including and especially yourself.

Who do you think you are? Do you think you are not good enough to be included, that God's children only include the "good ones"? Who do you think He did this all for? The imperfect ones, the flawed, the broken, the weak.

The plan of salvation is not a plan to save a group of good people. "[S]o by the obedience of one shall many be made righteous" (Romans 5:19). The beauty of His plan is it encompasses all, includes all, and belongs to all. Jesus Christ suffered all so He could save all of you and all of me. The lost sheep is found and belongs with the fold. You belong to this eternal family where God's love prevails. In His arms you belong.

You can be taught about the Atonement, but it will not become real until the day you truly need its healing power. Your path to get there may look different from mine, but healing comes from the same source and the same steps must be taken. In the end, it does the same for everyone. It heals and perfects the troubled soul. It brings change, forgiveness, and conversion.

Emilism: Remember Lot's wife. Do not look back!

"Believe in God; believe that he is, and that he created all things, both in heaven and in earth; believe that he has all wisdom, and all power, both in heaven and in earth" (Mosiah 4:9). A few concepts must be understood and applied before you can begin this journey of true healing, which builds a foundation both strong and steadfast. First, none of this will work unless you believe there is a God and that His character is defined by the tender love He has for His children.

Many victims, including myself, find it hard to trust men. This makes it difficult to consider reaching out to an Eternal Father. Knowing who He is will break down this barrier between a victim and the true source of healing—His love.

You can recognize God's character woven throughout the pages of the scriptures. The prophet Enos knew God would not lie. Mormon testified God is unchanging today and forever, and that He is a God of revelation, prophecies, and spiritual gifts. Moroni understood God's miracles will never cease. Abraham witnessed He is a God who keeps covenants. Nephi trusted and had faith God would always prepare a way for righteousness. Alma and Paul felt the transformation of God's great redeeming power. Joseph experienced the tender love of God when he was called by name and uniquely blessed (see Enos 1:6, Mormon 9:7-9, Moroni 7:29, Genesis 17, 1 Nephi 3:7, Mosiah 27:10-31, Acts 9, Joseph Smith History 1:17).

"Jesus saith unto him, I am the way, the truth, and the life: no man cometh unto the Father, but by me" (John 14:6). You can also recognize God's character through the life and teachings of His beloved son Jesus Christ, who came to do the Father's will. Jesus Christ was perfect, whole, and 100% united with our Father in Heaven. His will was the will of the Father.

Of the many magnificent purposes served in the life and ministry of the Lord Jesus Christ, one great aspect of that mission often goes uncelebrated. ... It is the grand truth that in all that Jesus came to say and do, including and especially

*in His atoning suffering and sacrifice, He was showing us
who and what God our Eternal Father is like, how
completely devoted He is to His children in every age and
nation. In word and in deed Jesus was trying to reveal and
make personal to us the true nature of His Father, our
Father in Heaven.*
Jeffrey R. Holland (19)

Scripture given in testimony of the Savior Jesus Christ could possibly be some of the most precious words written. They may only be words on a thin page, but they are woven with light and truth and connect as a candle in the night lighting the path to salvation.

Jesus Christ's humility and meekness emanate throughout as the scriptures give example after example of His love and of the healing power He possesses and bestows on every desiring heart. His sinless character allowed Him to teach the gospel and lead by perfection, which culminated in His great sacrifice as He gave His life for all the world.

God so loves us that He sent His Son, Jesus Christ, to be an example and provide us a way to find happiness in this life and in the next (see John 3:16). His work and glory is to bring to pass the eternal life of His children (see Moses 1:39).

The experiences I have had are unique to me but not unique to the nature of God. He is very much part of our lives. God is aware of, provides for, loves, and teaches all His children. The things we do may please or displease God, but will never change His unchanging love or the fact that He waits for any opportunity we give Him to bless us with that love.

The second thing you must believe in order to move forward is that change is real and change begins with you.

I've come to love a new beginning prompted by life's continuing changes. Lying dormant I'd never have a chance to admire the exotic bloom produced by a change in my orchid's chemistry. This change is what brought about the small green spike, giving a season of new life.

The sun rises in the morning and sheds light upon the earth. It promotes new growth and brings with it warmth and a new day. It chases the shadows away. I love the sound of snow melting off the roof in the spring time revealing dust the winter left behind and the rain that comes to wash it away. I even love the crisp mountain air of the fall telling me a long winter will be settling in.

The Atonement is eternal and is centered on the principle of eternal change: forsaking sin, healing sickness, mending broken hearts, and eternal progression. Both repentance and conversion include change—a change of heart and mind.

There are so many things people hold onto: anger, pride, fear, or hurt. This is not because they don't desire real change, but because letting go will make them vulnerable. Who would they be without these things? A stranger to themselves? They would have to be someone different, someone changed. The very idea of change can be overwhelming because of the amount of effort it requires.

If the way you live life is contingent on defining yourself as the victim, you will never know who you truly are.

You must, in a sense, make a sacrifice of your negative feelings to make room for the good with which God desires to bless you. "No man can serve two masters: for he will hate the one, and love the other; or else he will hold to the one, and despise the other. Ye cannot serve God and mammon" (Matthew 6:24). You cannot listen to the victim and the healer; love and hate, peace and conflict, happiness and sorrow, faith and fear cannot exist together.

What you allow to influence you will determine what you see and who you become. When you look at the world you must see it as a world of miracles where God knows no bounds for He is the creator of time and space and everything bends to His will. "For to be carnally minded is death; but to be spiritually minded is life and peace" (Romans 8:6).

If you learn to see through your spiritual eyes it will change everything about you, even your very presence on this earth. It will change how you think about yourself and others, the choices you make and the opportunities you have. Your spiritual eyes will open new paths and new opportunities. Your spiritual eyes will change you into someone with a legacy of faith that will be felt for generations to come.

> *Behold, when ye shall rend that veil of unbelief ... and blindness of mind, then shall the great and marvelous things which have been hid up from the foundation of the world from you—yea, when ye shall call upon the Father in my name, with a broken heart and a contrite spirit, ... then shall my revelations which I have caused to be written ... be unfolded in the eyes of all the people.*
> *Ether 4:15-16*

CHAPTER 18:

STEPS TO HEALING

How strong is your own testimony? Is it truly a sustaining power in your life, or is it more a hope that what you have learned is true? Is it more than a vague belief that worthwhile concepts and patterns of life seem to be reasonable and logical? Such mental assent will not help when you face the serious challenges that will inevitably come to you. Does your testimony guide you to correct decisions? To do so, fundamental truths must become part of the very fiber of your character. They must be an essential part of your being, more treasured than life itself.
Richard G. Scott (20)

Emilism: Your labor is not in vain.

There is a way to heal and proper steps to be taken. But because healing is not a straight path you will find these steps are like putting together the pieces of a puzzle. They are not lined up one by one, rather, each piece is searched out and carefully placed until the picture becomes clear.

STEP ONE: TELL YOUR SECRET

Emilism: Sometimes a kiss doesn't make it better and time does not heal the wound.

You don't have to be the victim anymore. You can escape the hell of non-growth. It doesn't matter if you tell one person or one hundred, you must first be willing to tell yourself. You can't heal what you don't know or don't acknowledge is broken.

Time to heal is needed, but merely the passage of time will not take care of a wound of this nature. Believing there is no real problem, that you can take care of it on your own, or that the effects will disappear in time, will only delay the healing process.

A willingness to have an honest heart, face the truth, and accept what comes next will begin the healing process, igniting your ability to tap into the power of the Atonement. As light and truth are shed upon your heart you will find this is not only the first step in the healing process, but the essence of the entire process, of every step.

Telling people you trust will give them the opportunity to understand you better and offer you the kind, caring attention you need. When people do not know the root of the problem they are confused by immature or destructive behaviors. This adds pressure and isolation and is often perceived as judgment.

Having open, honest discussions relieves the anxious mind and reveals where healing needs to take place.

If you choose not to tell, it is your right, but the consequences will be an unfulfilled life. It will leave a chasm of emptiness in your heart, restrict your ability to love and be loved, and prevent you from finding peace and healing. Ultimately you will be sacrificing your own happiness and quality of life. You may find courage knowing your disclosure will bring about necessary consequences for your abuser and protect future victims.

Part of telling the secret is deciding the appropriate people to tell and consider any legal involvement. Sexual abuse is a crime and in certain cases needs to be reported. This information should also come to the attention of anyone else who may have been exposed to the perpetrator. Seek out resources through your church or community. Healing can come in many forms. Different experiences that will speak to your heart and influence you. As you seek out available resources it is up to you to decide which will best support the healing you need.

In general people are ill-equipped to deal with or understand the effects of sexual abuse. Over the years, the best responses to my story were from those who were either trained to help victims or other victims who had also found healing. Other people try to fit this information into their own frame of reference so their reactions vary widely, but don't be surprised if you encounter opposition. This is difficult and sensitive information for people to take in. Most people simply do not know what to do with it.

Sexual abuse is a form of trauma. It stimulates emotions and physical reactions that are unnatural and drastically alter quality of life for years to come. It takes a lot of patience, love, and understanding to become a survivor. So realistically there are going to be some people who for various reasons cannot or do not want to be part of the healing process.

When sexual abuse happens within a family it adds a whole new dynamic, making it seem as though the victim is tearing the family apart. *"You're the one who told the secret. You're the one who made people choose sides. You're the one who created the divide and made people feel things they did not want to feel."* A family is torn by conflicting emotions of sadness, loyalty, shame, jealousy, love, or disappointment. I often felt the need to apologize to my family as if I had created this turmoil in their lives. In the beginning, I spent my time carrying the burden for others rather than on my own healing.

These feelings are not always exclusive to incestuous relationships. In any circumstance, you may wonder what you could or should have done differently, and if this guilt somehow makes the abuse your fault. This keeps you focused on pain from the past rather than on the healing the future can bring.

I know of several cases where a victim was told it was her fault or given partial blame because of how she was dressed or the late-night party she attended. This is wrong and such a notion should never be expressed.

It is not your fault. You do not have to feel guilt over the choices and feelings of the people around you. You cannot control the way people respond. In your search for healing it is key to remember to never internalize the weaknesses and mistakes of other people.

STEP TWO: MAKE YOUR SPIRITUALITY A PRIORITY

Emilism: Be the person God made.

Seek out counsel and guidance from a trusted spiritual advisor. This could be your pastor, priest, bishop, or other ecclesiastical leader. Ask for a priesthood blessing from someone you trust. Afterward write down the things that stood out to you in a journal. Maybe even use an audio recorder so you don't forget anything important (see LDS Handbook 2). There may be things you don't understand at first, but as you move forward you will understand and find guidance in the words delivered through the priesthood from your loving Heavenly Father.

Next, make your spirituality and healing process a priority. Remove destructive relationships from your life. Get yourself to a safe place if needed. Commit to daily prayer and scripture study. Get a journal and write in it. Organizing your thoughts onto paper can be a release. Don't be afraid to say whatever is in your heart. If later in your journey you find some of these thoughts to be painful or unproductive you may want to edit your journal or discard it. There is no rule a journal is written in stone. These records can evolve with you.

Have another journal to write down spiritual impressions and feelings you receive from the Holy Spirit. At first these promptings may be ever so quiet. Be patient. Light will grow and chase away the shadow of darkness. You will find great comfort and direction and be led to experiences God knows you need. Be present in church meetings even if you can barely get up the courage to go. Even if you don't feel it, there will be spiritual protection within those walls. Do not under any condition tell yourself that you are alone! I am here and you are reading this, so there is at least one person out there that makes you *not alone!*

STEP THREE: FIND RESTITUTION OF AGENCY AND SELF-WORTH

Emilism: I trust God more than men.

You can't be 100% united with God until you let go 100%. 99% is good, but it's not enough to make you whole. You can take steps while still holding onto your anger, pride, fear, and hurt. Each step will lead you down the path, but when you get to the end if you want to be completely whole you must take the plunge. Everything must go.

> *We tend to think of consecration only as yielding up, when divinely directed, our material possessions. But ultimate consecration is the yielding up of oneself to God. Heart, soul, and mind were the encompassing words of Christ in describing the first commandment, ... If kept, then our performances will, in turn, be fully consecrated for the lasting welfare of our souls. Such totality involves the submissive converging of feelings, thoughts, words, and deeds, the very opposite of estrangement.*
> *Neal A. Maxwell (21)*

I've watched many victims of sexual abuse, including myself, try to restore what has been taken by keeping control of their lives in precarious ways. Many turn to things like eating disorders, cutting, promiscuity, drugs, and/or alcohol. These self-destructive behaviors offer a sense of control but only mask the pain inside. This is exactly what I did through my bulimia. While binging and purging might seem like out of control behaviors, they made it possible for me to avoid thinking about the pain and rejection. There were times I thought I had gained control over my bulimia, just to find myself back at the toilet relieving my stress.

Some hold onto their trials, replaying them over and over to gain sympathy from others and influence the way people perceive them. Some will bury them deep within as a way to control the victim inside, never to rear its ugly head. This is also an attempt to control the way others perceive them as they are afraid to be labeled a victim. Those who turn to drugs and/or alcohol control feelings by finding a way to numb the pain. Some turn to sex to prove they have gained control over their own sexuality in spite of what has happened. Those who turn to cutting or eating disorders transfer the pain to another focal point. All of these things are attempts to gain power by having control over some aspect of their lives.

Fear keeps you trapped in these behaviors—fear of what people will think or say, how they will react, fear of facing the pain and the work it takes to heal, fear of putting your trust in God, fear of taking that leap of faith and nothing being there to catch you. Fear of fear shuts down your power and puts up walls, handing this precious power over to the Adversary. "For God hath not given us the spirit of fear; but of power, and of love, and of a sound mind" (2 Timothy 1:7). Fear is the root of destruction and the opposite of faith.

Being a victim of sexual abuse robs you of your power and control. Ironically, continuing to let yourself be the victim through any of these behaviors does the same. They will not give you power or control. In fact, they suck away even more of these precious gifts. The Adversary would love to see you bury yourself deep in these things, thus creating even more distance between you and the ability to heal.

There is only one way to restore the lost power and control. It is by exercising your freedom to make emotionally healthy decisions. Using your freedom, whether in large or small ways, is your greatest power.

STEP FOUR: PUT YOUR TRUST IN GOD

Emilism: Do not let God be your last resort.

Your joy is contingent upon your ability to trust. So think of it on a scale. I love math because, just like the gospel, if you follow the formula you will always get the right answer. However happy you want to be, that is how much trust you must put in Him.

> *Come unto me, all ye that labour and are heavy laden, and I will give you rest. Take my yoke upon you, and learn of me; for I am meek and lowly in heart: and ye shall find rest unto your souls. For my yoke is easy and my burden is light.*
> *Matthew 11:28-30.*

The dependency you should seek is a partnership with God, an *interdependence*, to be 100% united with Him, to be yoked together, pulling together, side by side. Faith is your part and grace is His.

Although He can make the way light, your effort is necessary as you push forward paving the path together. He will give you strength beyond your own, but as you move along you will also build your own strength, character, and testimony.

This life is meant to be a period of preparation where we, through trial, come to know and understand God (see Alma 34:32). But this preparation is also meant to bring joy (see 2 Nephi 2:25). So the true challenge is to find joy in the journey, and joy will be yours if you obey Him and learn and live His commandments.

"Trust in the Lord with all thine heart; and lean not unto thine own understanding. In all thy ways acknowledge him, and he shall direct thy paths" (Proverbs 3:5-6). It takes trust to follow your spiritual eyes not knowing where they may lead. It takes faith to act not knowing what you will gain in return. It takes courage to stand not knowing if you will stand alone. You must put your trust, faith, and courage to work, letting God lead you and letting Him stand beside you.

STEP FIVE: DRAW CLOSE TO GOD TO FEEL HIS LOVE

Emilism: Suffer with Him and become heirs.

Even small expressions of love, when accompanied by an honest heart, can lead to big changes.

The Cycle of God's Love: The Atonement at Work

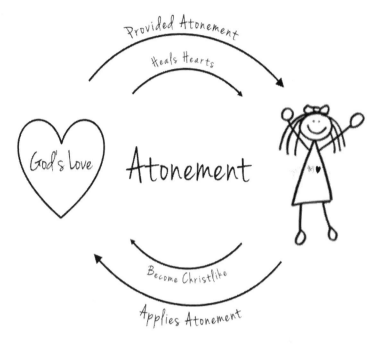

> For God so loved the world, that he gave his only begotten Son, that whosoever believeth in him should not perish, but have everlasting life (John 3:16).

Because God loves His children, He provided an Atonement whereby they could be made perfect and return to live with Him, and so they could find peace and happiness while on this earth.

> And thou shalt love the Lord thy God with all thy heart, and with all thy soul, and with all thy mind, and with all thy strength: this is the first commandment (Mark 12:30).

Your love for God will develop a desire in your heart to learn and live His commandments. Your choice to dedicate yourself to Him ignites the power of the Atonement in your life.

➢ *But unto you that fear my name shall the Sun of righteousness arise with healing in his wings (Malachi 4:2).*

As you show your love for God by keeping the commandments and remaining dedicated to Him, He will provide experiences that will fill your soul with His love, putting the Atonement into action. In each healing moment, you will witness God's power and learn who you are and what your divine nature is.

➢ *And above all these things put on charity, which is the bond of perfectness (Colossians 3:14).*

As you draw closer to God you will be made whole, piece by piece, experience upon experience, until you become Christlike emulating His love. The charity you have developed in your heart will solidify your transformation in the Atonement.

The love of God for His children is most profoundly
expressed in His gift of Jesus as our Redeemer. ... To
partake of the love of God is to partake of Jesus' Atonement
and the emancipations and joys which it can bring.
Neal A. Maxwell (22)

STEP SIX: FORGIVE THE PERPETRATOR

Emilism: Forgiveness is the gift for doing the work.

This is an important point. It is an obstacle I faced for years and affects every victim of abuse. Forgiveness stems from love, so how can someone who does not know love, who has shut down emotion and been stripped of self-worth possibly forgive?

So much of my identity and self-worth was tied up in the perpetrator. Could I choose to forgive the person who stole my ability to choose? Ultimately, yes, but first my agency had to be restored. The path to forgiveness is found in the process of healing.

> *And now, my brethren, I desire that ye shall plant this word in your hearts, and as it beginneth to swell even so nourish it by your faith. And behold, it will become a tree, springing up in you unto everlasting life. And then may God grant unto you that your burdens may be light, through the joy of his Son. And even all this can ye do if ye will. Amen.*
> *Alma 33:23*

There are many things you can simply let go of, but a situation as significant as abuse takes a journey to find forgiveness. This scripture in Alma describes the journey: plant the seed of belief, nourish it, have faith, it will grow into something beautiful, then the burden will be lifted. Forgiveness at last.

Having a testimony of forgiveness is something that can't be explained until you have it, but when you do you will recognize it as a unique gift. I have heard other testimonies of the feelings forgiveness brings, but those words only resonate with people who have made the journey and been put to the test. When your healing process is complete, you can forgive completely.

Because it is a commandment, it is our job to seek true forgiveness, and it is God's job to deal with justice. Only He knows how to deal lovingly and justly with His children. God's work is to save souls, not to condemn them. He wants us to seek forgiveness because He knows the blessings and freedom it brings. By pridefully thinking you are the better person by forgiving through your own good graces, you have missed the mark. It has not healed you or helped the other person. True forgiveness is born of Christlike love.

Forgiving someone does not mean it is appropriate to put yourself in the path of danger. You can be filled with charity towards others and still set boundaries for emotionally healthy relationships.

STEP SEVEN: ENDURE TO THE END

Emilism: Live in your weakness, but not of your weakness.

We cannot be perfect here and now, but we can be 100% united with God if all our gaps are filled. What I mean is that if you are willing to give your whole heart to God and make the effort necessary to move through the refining process of the Atonement, then you will, step by step, be united with Him.

Through each step, you will discover who you are by discovering who God is and His plan for you. Then when you are 100% united with Him you will be made whole and find your happy ending.

Although progression never really ends and mortal life continues to bring trials, this happy ending will be an end to your suffering, the moment you realize you are not alone. Then you will know with 100% surety that the power of God is real. Then, when your faith and trust are complete, the doors of heaven will be open to you.

> *Just before the Savior carried out the Atonement, ... He pled*
> *for unity: "That they all may be one; as thou, Father, are in*
> *me, and I in thee, that they also may be one in us: that the*
> *world may believe that thou hast sent me" (John17:21).*
> *From this prayer we learn how the gospel unites us with*
> *Heavenly Father and Jesus Christ and with each other.*
> *When we live the gospel, receiving the saving ordinances and*
> *keeping our covenants, our natures are changed. The*
> *Savior's Atonement sanctifies us, and we can live in unity,*
> *enjoying peace in this life and preparing to dwell with the*
> *Father and his Son forever.*
> *True to the Faith (23)*

This is not about giving up on who you are. Or giving up on hope. Or thinking your progression is done. Being 100% is about finding your best self. Paul's wise words were, "[F]or when I am weak, then am I strong" (2 Corinthians 12:10).

Being 100% means accepting the plan 100%, the ups and the downs. But the ups and downs can happen around you instead of inside you. While trials may still come, you get better at trusting God, you get better at having faith and letting go. You get better at recognizing God's hand in your life and His direction.

You acknowledge your weaknesses in order to gain Christlike qualities. In recognizing your weaknesses, you are humble enough to turn to others and to the Savior for help. There you will find strength and a place to chase away your fears. You magnify your strengths and talents in order to serve others and fulfill your unique divine mission. Your service will add harmony to God's plan. Your love of God and others will give your life purpose and allow the Atonement to continue to work for you.

Being 100% is ultimately about relief: relief of guilt, fear, anxiety and future distress, and those feelings being replaced with peace, gratitude, hope, strength, and confidence.

I've found often the most difficult of life's trials revolve around the deepest yearnings of our hearts. We must live in this world to be tried and tested. Here, you will always be subject to the weaknesses and frailties of mortality, but you do not have to let those things dictate your behavior or who you are. As you develop your divine nature you can be a light amidst the darkness. Then you are no longer the victim. Then you are free.

These steps are not meant to feel easy, but they are meant to feel sure. The prize is worth the work. It is done one step at a time. Humble prayer will facilitate each essential step. As a prerequisite to forgiveness there must first be a desire for peace, a spiritual connection with God, and then acknowledgement of His love. The next step is to let go and put your trust in Him. As you do this your agency and self-worth will be restored. Thanks to the ransom paid by the Atonement of Jesus Christ, full forgiveness can be extended and maintained for those who will endure to the end.

Emilism: The Spirit will be there to comfort if you only ask.

I'm not going to lie. This process takes a lot of work and a lot of patience. You don't want your effort to be in vain, so here's how to make sure the work is working for you.

There is one simple solution and this is the only time I will tell you to do this: look back. Look back and see the results. Look for where and when God has shaped you. Look how far you have come. These little changes happen almost imperceptibly. They take time and patience to develop. That is why, although you should not linger in the past, you must look back. The more you look for the hand of God, the more your spiritual eyes will reveal His influence. This is a huge part of moving forward.

> *Before I would write, I would ponder this question: "Have I seen the hand of God reaching out to touch us or our children or our family today?" As I kept at it, something began to happen. As I would cast my mind over the day, I would see evidence of what God had done for one of us that I had not recognized in the busy moments of the day. As that happened, and it happened often, I realized that trying to remember had allowed God to show me what He had done.*
> *Henry B. Eyring (24)*

Organize your thoughts in your mind and put them to words in your journal. When you write your testimony of the work you have done and the results that have come, the Spirit will confirm to you that it is true and solidify that step towards the Atonement in your heart.

Emilism: Life doesn't get easier, you just get better!

There will be times when you feel distant, almost forsaken. Be grateful for the times the Spirit comforts you. Be filled with hope and gratitude enough to keep your thoughts positive and your heart full.

People tend to think of God's guidance as being accompanied by positive feelings, but sometimes it doesn't feel good. At times, God will push and pull, manipulating your life as an artist would with a lump of clay, trying to shape and mold it into something priceless. "Nevertheless the Lord seeth fit to chasten his people; yea, he trieth their patience and their faith" (Mosiah 23:21). God will allow his children to experience negative feelings to strengthen and prepare them for future blessings and understanding He desires to bestow.

When discouragement comes, you must push aside the feelings of doubt and pain. It's in these moments you will make the choice about who you want to be. These are the moments you will have to dig deep to dig out. Don't spend time thinking about who you wish you were or where you wish you could be. Instead focus on what is happening inside your heart. Assess where your spiritual needs are and attend to them. These are the moments that will define the outcome of your life.

[W]e glory in tribulations also: knowing that tribulation
worketh patience; And patience, experience; and experience,
hope: And hope maketh not ashamed; because the love of
God is shed abroad in our hearts by the Holy Ghost which
is given unto us.
Romans 5:3-5

These principles Paul highlighted are the building blocks of change. As you pass through tribulation, you gain patience, experience, and restored hope. This hope is what keeps you moving forward. Hope for a better future, hope for healing, hope for peace, for God's love, or for answers to prayers.

Hope for happiness was what influenced all of my decisions. This honest and deep desire was what drew me back each time I felt discouraged. "For we are saved by hope: but hope that is seen is not hope: ... But if we hope for that we see not, *then* do we with patience wait for *it*" (Romans 8:24-25). You may not be able to see the end of the path, but each step is paved with hope. This is where the Atonement takes effect, using your life experiences to shape and mold the person you will become.

Even if all you have right now is hope that you will make it to your happy ending, let that guide your way. God will grant unto you according to your honest desire. Obstacles may come, challenges may pull you down, and weaknesses may feel suffocating, but these things may be swept out of the way. For the honest in heart there is always a path out of darkness.

Emilism: Don't be afraid to give.

I have laid out the steps needed to get to this point. Now it is up to you to endure to the end and it must become your own story. Do not check out of your healing process. Be present. You must keep your promise to remain dedicated to God and keep a habit of doing the Sunday School answers: study your scriptures, say your prayers, and attend your meetings. If you are present in your meetings, in your thoughts and in your heart, then lessons from the Spirit will come to light your way.

Remember healing is not a single event, but many moments that take place in honest hearts and add up to one big change.

I could write page after page about God's great love for you and all His children, but it won't make a bit of difference until you discover it for yourself. As I said in the beginning the discovery of my life has been that His children are His treasure. But your discovery of this knowledge must come from your own search. It is a personal experience between you and your Father in Heaven. I can only say pretty words that might get you curious enough to search it out. I have given many hints as to what God's love feels like, what to search for, and how. This is not an easy process, but you have now made your first step on a long journey.

AFTERWORD

Emilism: I used to be fed with crumbs, now I am fed with feasts.

Whether big or small my Emilisms have been my guide and compass, they are my inner voice, or the light of Christ. Life is full of spiritual truisms to be discovered. They are eternal truths, found in the scriptures and the words of the prophets. Elder Richard G. Scott (20) said:

> *In this uncertain world, there are some things that never change: the perfect love of our Heavenly Father for each of us; the assurance that He is there and will always hear us; the existence of absolute, unchanging truths; the fact that there is a plan of happiness; the assurance that success in life is attained through faith in Jesus Christ and obedience to His teachings because of the redemptive power of His Atonement; the certainty of life after death; the reality that our condition there is set by how we live here.*

Say what you will about the weaknesses of men, about the person at church who offended you, or the program that was not put together right; that has nothing to do with the eternal truths the gospel of Jesus Christ teaches. The church organization exists for one purpose, to build your relationship with God and His Son, Jesus Christ, who will redeem. In weakness some may overlook or misrepresent the gospel, but that does not change the reality that these principles are true and eternal.

God is our father. He loves us. He will provide all that we need to become exalted, including letting us pass through trial. With all God's power and all that He has to offer, He can do nothing for us unless we use our agency to choose it. His miracles are happening: be present, pay attention, keep a journal, you will see.

I know God lives and that Jesus Christ is His only begotten Son. I know He did come to this earth to save and redeem souls. I know it now more than I have ever known. This knowledge has taken root and grown throughout my soul connecting my heart, spirit, and mind. Writing this book has been the therapy I never had. It has changed my life. It is a gift of love that God has helped me unwrap piece by piece, and now it is my gift to give.

ACKNOWLEDGEMENTS

I believe Tom is my soulmate in that God intended us to be together. There is no one else in the world with which I could have made this deep loving connection. He is the only man I have ever loved. He is the complete opposite in personality. Together we make quite the pair, but together I know we can help each other grow to our full potential, which is how marriage should be. I love that he loves me. He makes me laugh, he pushes me out of my comfort zone, he takes care of me in every way. He has always believed in me, long before I believed in myself. He is the reason I began to believe in myself. I love to remember sitting in the celestial room in the San Diego temple, just the two of us alone, the sun shining on his freckles, waiting to be sealed for time and all eternity.

I love my parents and I know they love me. I believe there is a purpose and a plan for me as their daughter. I appreciate that even when life has been hard, they remain dedicated to each other and to the gospel. I am grateful for the love they provide me. I am grateful to be born in the covenant and under the protection that provides. The path through life is not easy for anyone, but my parents did provide me with all I needed to find my way and make my own choices. They are good and honest, and I love them.

My best friend and cousin, my sister soulmate. Proof that you don't need to walk the same path in life to learn the same lessons. We have been on completely different paths, yet spiritually we have taken the same road and come to the same conclusions. She is my confidant. She is more loyal than anyone I have ever known. She is funny and loves people in the most genuine way. She is a true friend through and through to everyone she meets. She has a strong testimony and I know I can trust her with anything. She is beautiful. She is a light in my life. I believe God put us in the same family and brought our lives together for a greater purpose than I know right now.

A beautiful arrangement of my favorite hymn, "Nearer Dear Savior to Thee", is available at rebeccabelliston.com. Rebecca Belliston graciously wrote this piano solo as a companion to *Restoring Virtue*.

GLOSSARY OF LDS TERMINOLOGY

Atonement: "The word *atone* means to reconcile, or to restore to harmony. Through the Atonement of Jesus Christ, we can be reconciled to our Heavenly Father. We can ultimately dwell in His presence forever, having been 'made perfect through Jesus'" (25) (see 2 Nephi 2:5-10).

Adversary: Also called Satan or the devil is the enemy of righteousness (See Revelation 12:9, 2 Nephi 2:27).

Baptism: Ordinance performed by priesthood authority in which a person is immersed in water and symbolically pronounced clean. Through baptism a person becomes a member of The Church of Jesus Christ of Latter-day Saints.

Bishop: The ecclesiastical leader of a local church congregation (ward). Equivalent of a priest or pastor. In the LDS church the bishop is a lay minister.

Book of Mormon: Another testament of Jesus Christ. An account written by ancient prophets of Jesus Christ's ministry to the people on the American continent.

Calling: Originates from the idea that a person is "called of God" to serve in His kingdom. Each member is given an assignment from his/her bishop through inspiration. Callings are accepted voluntarily.

Celestial room: A room found in LDS temples symbolizing the exalted state of living in the presence of Heavenly Father and His Son Jesus Christ.

Disciplinary action: Priesthood leaders are responsible to compassionately help a person turn away from behaviors that prevent them from progressing.

Fast and testimony meeting: The first Sunday of every month church services are open to the congregation for those who would like to bear testimony specifically of the restored gospel of Jesus Christ and His atoning sacrifice.

Holy Ghost: A personage of spirit, without a body of flesh and bones. Works in unity with God and Jesus Christ to teach the truth of all things.

Personal Progress: A six-year program for young women ages 12-18 dedicated to building life skills, setting goals, and strengthening faith.

Priesthood: Power and authority of God. In mortality, this power is given to men for the authority to act in God's name.

Priesthood blessing: Given by the laying on of hands and through inspiration in the form of a prayer. Blessings are given to one who is sick, in need of special counsel, comfort, healing, or to set apart a new calling.

Priesthood leader: A priesthood leader is given stewardship and responsibility, within a specific calling, to administer or attend to the spiritual and temporal needs of members.

Primary: Program for the religious instruction and activity of children ages 18 months-12 years old.

Prophet: President and priesthood leader at the head of the church. Only man inspired to speak for the Lord as a prophet, seer, and revelator for the whole world.

Relief Society: Organization for women ages 18 and up. Dedicated to strengthening faith, compassionate service, and church welfare. Ward relief society leadership is made up of a president, two counselors, and a secretary.

Repentance: A change of heart.

Sealing or being sealed (eternal marriage): Ordinance performed in LDS temples uniting husband and wife, or children and their parents, for time and all eternity. Sealing ordinance is what allows families to be reunited beyond the grave.

Sealing room: A room in the temple designated to perform the sealing ordinance. In this room, mirrors are hung on opposite walls—their repeated reflection representing families joined together for eternity.

Seminary: Weekday scripture study class for high school age kids.

Spirit daughter: The plan of salvation, or plan of happiness, teaches we are eternal beings, spirit children of an eternal God. Before we came to earth we lived in His presence. We chose to come to this earth where we would gain a physical body and learn to choose between good and evil. By accepting the Atonement of Jesus Christ, we can be made perfect and again return to God's presence.

Stake: Group of 5-12 wards under the same area priesthood leadership.

Stake President: Area church authority, priesthood leader, that presides over a group of 5-12 wards.

Sustain: Each calling is given a sustaining vote from the congregation who commit to offer support, help, and prayers when needed.

Temple: Special church building dedicated to making covenants, performing ordinances, and receiving promised blessings. The sealing ordinance is performed in the temple.

Tender mercy: Compassionate treatment of a person greater than what is deserved and is part of the enabling power of Jesus Christ.

Testimony: A spiritual witness given by the power of the Holy Ghost.

Testimony meeting: In lieu of assigned speakers, the first Sunday of each month is set aside for members of the congregation to voluntarily share their testimonies of Jesus Christ.

Visiting teacher: A woman assigned to watch over, spiritually uplift, and help another woman in her congregation. Usually two visiting teachers are assigned to each woman.

Ward: Local geographically organized church congregation. A bishop presides over each ward.

Young Single Adult Ward: Congregation made up of singles ages 18-30.

Young Women Advisor: In the Young Women (or youth group) program three advisors are assigned to each age group: 12-13 years old, 14-15 years old, 16-17 years old.

Young Women President: Presides over youth group program for girls ages 12-17 years old. Works with two counselors, one secretary, and three advisors.

REFERENCES

1. Wirthlin, Joseph B. "Concern for the One", Salt Lake City UT. April 2008. *Lds.org*. Web. 1 May 2015. <https://www.lds.org/general-conference/2008/04/concern-for-the-one?lang=eng>

2. Uchtdorf, Dieter F. "Continue in Patience", Salt Lake City UT. April 2010. *Lds.org*. 1 May 2015. <https://www.lds.org/general-conference/2010/04/continue-in-patience?lang=eng>

3. Edgley, Richard C. "Faith—the Choice is Yours", Salt Lake City UT. October 2010. *Lds.org*. 1 May 2015. <https://www.lds.org/general-conference/2010/10/faith-the-choice-is-yours?lang=eng>

4. Holland, Jeffrey R. "The Inconvenient Messiah", Provo UT. February 1984. *Lds.org*. 1 May 2015. <https://www.lds.org/ensign/1984/02/the-inconvenient-messiah?lang=eng>

5. Holland, Jeffrey R. "The Best Is Yet to Be", Provo UT. January 2010. *Lds.org*. 1 May 2015. <https://www.lds.org/ensign/2010/01/the-best-is-yet-to-be?lang=eng>

6. Scott, Richard G. "To Acquire Spiritual Guidance", Provo UT. October 2009. *Lds.org*. 1 May 2015. <https://www.lds.org/general-conference/2009/10/to-acquire-spiritual-guidance?lang=eng>

7. Allred, Silvia H. "Charity Never Faileth", Salt Lake City UT. October 2011. *Lds.org*. 1 May 2015.

<https://www.lds.org/general-conference/2011/10/charity-never-faileth?lang=eng>

8. Monson, Thomas S. "What Have I Done for Someone Today?", Salt Lake City UT. October 2009. *Lds.org*. 1 May 2015. <https://www.lds.org/general-conference/2009/10/what-have-i-done-for-someone-today?lang=eng>

9. Scott, Richard G. "To Be Healed", Salt Lake City UT. April 1994. *Lds.org*. Web. 1 May 2015. <https://www.lds.org/general-conference/2001/04/plow-in-hope?lang=eng>

10. Maxwell, Neal A. "Plow in Hope", Salt Lake City UT. April 2001. *Lds.org*. Web. 1 May 2015. <https://www.lds.org/general-conference/2001/04/plow-in-hope?lang=eng>

11. Kimball, Spencer. *The Miracle of Forgiveness*. Salt Lake City: Bookcraft, 1969. 363. Print.

12. Eyring, Henry B. "That We May Be One", Salt Lake City UT. April 1998. *Lds.org*. Web. 1 May 2015. <https://www.lds.org/ensign/1998/05/that-we-may-be-one?lang=eng>

13. Uchtdorf, Dieter F. "Your Happily Ever After", Salt Lake City UT. April 2010. *Lds.org*. Web. 1 May 2015. <https://www.lds.org/general-conference/2010/04/your-happily-ever-after?lang=eng>

14. Monson, Thomas S. "Precious Children—A Gift from God", Salt Lake City UT. October 1991. *Lds.org*. Web. 1 May 2015. <https://www.lds.org/general-conference/1991/10/precious-children-a-gift-from-god?lang=eng>

15. "Child Sexual Abuse Statistics." *The National Center for Victims of Crime*. National Center for Victims of Crime, 2012. Web. 1 May 2015. <http://victimsofcrime.org/media/reporting-on-child-sexual-abuse/child-sexual-abuse-statistics>

16. Hinckley, Gordon B. *Standing for Something*. New York: Three Rivers, 2000. 158. Print.

17. Christofferson, D. Todd. "The Moral Force of Women", Salt Lake City UT. October 2013. *Lds.org*. Web. 1 May 2015.

<https://www.lds.org/general-conference/2013/10/the-moral-force-of-women?lang=eng>

18. Benson, Ezra T. "Born of God", Salt Lake City UT. October 1985. *Lds.org.* Web. 1 May 2015. <https://www.lds.org/general-conference/1985/10/born-of-god?lang=eng>

19. Holland, Jeffrey R. "The Grandeur of God", Salt Lake City UT. October 2003. *Lds.org.* Web. 1 May 2015. <https://www.lds.org/general-conference/2003/10/the-grandeur-of-god?lang=eng>

20. Scott, Richard G. "The Power of a Strong Testimony", Salt Lake City UT. October 2001. *Lds.org.* Web. 1 May 2015. <https://www.lds.org/general-conference/2001/10/the-power-of-a-strong-testimony?lang=eng>

21. Maxwell, Neal A. "Consecrate Thy Performance", Salt Lake City UT. April 2002. *Lds.org.* Web. 1 May 2015. <https://www.lds.org/general-conference/2002/04/consecrate-thy-performance?lang=eng>

22. Maxwell, Neal A. "Lessons from Laman and Lemuel", Salt Lake City UT. October 1999. *Lds.org.* Web. 1 May 2015. <https://www.lds.org/general-conference/1999/10/lessons-from-laman-and-lemuel?lang=eng>

23. "Unity." *True To The Faith*. Salt Lake City: The Church of Jesus Christ of Latter-day Saints, 2004. 182-183. Print.

24. Eyring, Henry B. "O, Remember, Remember", Salt Lake City UT. October 2007. *Lds.org.* Web. 1 May 2015. <https://www.lds.org/general-conference/2007/10/o-remember-remember?lang=eng>

25. "Atonement of Jesus Christ." *True To The Fatih*. Salt Lake City. The Church of Jesus Christ of Latter-day Saints, 2004. 14-21. Print

ABOUT THE AUTHOR

Emily Hope is a wife, a mother, a daughter, and a friend.

She enjoys cold weather, which is why she lives in the beautiful
state of Alaska.

She loves biking, picking berries in the wild Alaskan frontier,
discount movies with her best friend, sharing spiritual
experiences with her children, and the comfort of
her husband's hugs.

Emily is a member of the Church of Jesus Christ of Latter-day
Saints.

Her life is blessed in more ways than she can count.

Visit www.restoring-virtue.com or
find Restoring Virtue on Facebook.

Made in United States
Orlando, FL
04 May 2023

32806502R00104